EPHESIANS

"Key-Words of the Inner Life"

F. B. Meyer

CHRISTIAN LITERATURE CRUSADE

FORT WASHINGTON   PENNSYLVANIA 19034

CHRISTIAN LITERATURE CRUSADE
Fort Washington, Pennsylvania 19034

CANADA
Box 189, Elgin, Ontario KOG 1EO

This edition 1982
under special arrangement with
the British publisher.

ISBN-87508-344-7

PRINTED IN U.S.A.

EPHESIANS

By the same Author

ABRAHAM

PAUL

PETER

THE WAY INTO THE HOLIEST

Preface

Repeated perusal of the Books of Scripture, and especially of the Epistles, will enable the devout student to detect certain words, which keep recurring, like a note or chord struck repeatedly in a musical composition. One of the most interesting and instructive methods of studying Scripture is with this aim in view. In the present case, it has been applied to the EPISTLE TO THE EPHESIANS with the following result.

The Epistle to the Ephesians is pre-eminently the Epistle of the Inner Life. It is not astonishing, therefore, to find that its characteristic key-words are also the key-words of the Inner Life. And in proportion as we weave them into the texture of our life, we shall become possessed of the tenderness and strength, the depth of knowledge and height of communion, which have endeared this Epistle to all ages of the church.

It has not been possible, in these narrow limits, to attempt a full Exposition of these marvellous words, aglow with heaven's altar-flame. But sufficient has been said to show its rich lodes of ore, and their direction, and the method by which they may be carried into currency for daily living.

F. B. MEYER

Contents

I

The Father

Ephesians 1:2.

We need both *Grace* and *Peace*. Grace to help in our times of need; Peace to keep our heart and mind. The one as the blue vault of Heaven above us, with its smile of sun, and breath of air, and reviving rain; the other as the blue depths of the ocean, tranquil and calm. But neither of these blessed gifts can be ours till we have come to recognise God as our Father. Be doubtful about that, and you will not dare to exercise the child's privilege of claiming what you want from the Father's stores; and you will miss the unspeakable rest which breathes through the heart of the child, as it nestles to the father's side. Open your heart to the Spirit of Adoption that He may flutter, dove-like, into its depths; and, in the cry Abba, bear witness with your spirit that you are a child of God, and if a child, then a participator in his Grace and Peace.

1:3.

It was thus that Jesus lived.

There was no lack of either Grace or Peace in his human life, because He dwelt ever in the bosom of the Father. He spake no word, and wrought no deed of mercy, that was not derived from his Father. He refused to make one stone into bread, because so sure that his Father could not forget Him, but knew just what was needed for the body which He had provided for Him. The often up-turned eye witnessed to the attitude of his spirit. There was never a film of separation or cloud of misunderstanding, Jesus did always those things which pleased Him. "Even so, Father," was the whisper with which He met all the incidents of his life, whether cloud or sun.

Let us learn to live thus towards the God and Father of our Lord Jesus Christ. There must always be an impassable gulf between His relationship to the Father and ours. But, withal, there are points of contact. He waits to reveal to us the Father, according to His own words (Matt. 11:27). He longs to reproduce in us, by the Holy Ghost, His own spirit on Sonship, and to bring us to know His Father as our Father, His God as ours. There is no joy, which more satisfies His soul for its travail, than that His own should come so to know the name and character of His Father, and so abide in it, as that the love with which the Father loved Him, may be in them as a warm and blessed experience. When this purpose is accomplished in us, our Marahs will be turned to Elims; and we shall be full of peace, since our Father has mixed our cups, appointed our paths, set our life-tasks, and whispers to our secret hearts that He is well pleased with us in Jesus.

1:17.

Our Father is the Father of Glory.

Do we enough consider the glory of our relationship? Are we not apt to become so familiar with the thought of God as not sufficiently to consider the majesty of His nature, or the wonderful advantages that must accrue to those who know Him as their Father? All that He was to Jesus, He is willing to be to us; and all that He has He is willing to place at the disposal of our faith. Think, O tried and straightened soul, that God loves thee and watches thee, as no father ever loved or watched the helpless babe given him from the dying hand of his young and passionately-loved wife. Remember, too, His wealth as the Father of Glory. All beings in all worlds, all worlds in all spheres, all spheres in all ages, wait his word: be still and trust! Men and things could have no power against thee, except it were given them from above; their power is controlled by the Father's care; there is a thus-far beyond which they cannot go: and it is through them that the Father is bringing you, as one of his many sons, to glory. May He give you the spirit of wisdom and revelation, and open the eyes of your heart that you may know Him!

2:18.

Access to the Father.

Prayer assumes a new complexion so soon as we properly appreciate God's Fatherliness. Granted that it must always be through Jesus, and by the Holy Spirit, yet, ultimately, it is access to the Father. The first thought of a little child in any need is *Mother, Father.* There is instant movement of eyes, and feet, and voice, towards the one dear source of help and comfort. And so, when we have learnt to know the Father, as revealed in Jesus, our heart will be constantly going out towards Him. The Father's heart has twelve gates, that one of them may be contiguous to every conceivable position in which His children may be placed. Of course there will be times when we shall deliberately bow our knees unto the Father; but there will be many more when we shall have access to Him in a swift-winged thought, a tear hastily brushed away, a yearning, an ejaculation, a loving, restful glance of mutual understanding. Strange that we make so little of these wonderful opportunities of access to the Father!

3 : 14, 15.

All the fatherhoods of earth derive their meaning and value from the great Fatherhood.

As the Tabernacle, with its sashes, cords, and curtains, was an embodiment of things in the heavens; so the homes of men are intended to represent aspects and conceptions of that love, which can be set forth by no one phase of human affection, but combines in itself, mother, father, brother, sister, lover, loved. The tenderest, noblest home-life is, at the best, but "broken light"; and yet it is a type, an emblem, an embodiment of God's love to us, its proto-type and ideal. Were you the nursling of a blessed home, receding far away in the vista of the past? Transfer its memories to the present, and know that they live still as facts in your relationship to God. And you, who never knew a home-life that you care to recall, be sure that the tenderest that man ever knew is not to be compared with that in which you are living, if only you knew it.

4 : 5,6.

The one fatherhood makes the one brotherhood and sisterhood.

To have been born of the same parents constitutes a

bond of union between those of the most diverse temperaments and tastes. The variety becomes a true unity, and gives a flavour of keen interest to the life of the household. Nothing in this world is more beautiful than the play of life in the home where the babe and the young student, the merry boy and the thoughtful, earnest maiden blend. This also is a pattern of things in the heavens. Because there is one God and Father of all who are in Christ, over them to cover their heads in the day of battle; through them, as the breath of the wind murmuring through the many pipes of nature's organ; and in them as the source of their life—they are all one in Him.

5 : 20.

Let us then give thanks always for all things to the Father.

I have a beloved friend, who has made it the habit of her life to obey this injunction literally. When her husband's factory was in flames, when her children were pronounced to be seriously ill, and when other apparent disasters befell her, she went alone into her chamber, and knelt down to thank God for all, because she knew that He was a Father still; that He loved her too well to give her anything but the best; and that He must love her very much to be willing to bless her at the cost of so much pain. We may not always *feel* like thanking God for all things; but let us always will and dare to do it. Let us not look at the providence, but at the Father behind it. Let us not examine the crate, but let us search within for the gift of love. Though at first sight we may be disappointed and sad, whatever the Father sends must be the very best. Dare to believe it, and you will come to find it so.

6:23.

And thus we shall learn to receive and know the Father's peace.

The very peace that fills His own glorious nature—the peace which, in the experience of human hearts, is so closely allied with love and faith, the peace of the Lord Jesus Christ—will settle down upon the troubled, restless heart, as the evening, with its cool air and majestic beauty, settles on the fevered landscape.

2

The Father's Wealth

The Epistle to the Ephesians is full of the wealth of God's nature. It is set to that master-chord struck centuries before by a temple minstrel, "Thou, Lord, art good, and ready to forgive; and *plenteous in mercy* unto all those that call upon Thee." The apostle struggles with the inadequacy of human language in his attempt to convey some conception of what God is willing to expend upon the heirs of salvation.

We are all familiar with God's prodigality in Nature. Every common hedgerow with its wealth of vegetation; every lazy trout-stream, where the fish lie in the cool depths, and the flowers dip down their dainty cups; every square foot of the midnight sky, set thick with rare jewels —attest the unsearchable resources of his power. But these are for all the world to see. And as the man of wealth opens richer stores to those that share his love than he displays to the casual visitor, so God has prepared for those that love Him, things which eye hath not seen, nor ear heard, nor the heart of man conceived. There are riches of grace in the heart of God, of forgiveness, and pitifulness, and mercy, of which the foremost of the saints in the heavenly ranks, and the chief of sinners on earth—however heavily they have drawn on them—know comparatively nothing. We have no standard for computing infinity; and infinity is the orbit in which God lives and loves.

This is what the apostle means when he speaks of the riches of God's Grace.

1:7.

Our trespasses are forgiven, according to the riches of God's grace.

"Trespass" is the term used by our Lord of the negligences, sins, and ignorances, which mark the lives even of those who can look up into God's face and say, *Our Father.* The conjunction *and* which links the prayer for the forgiveness of these with the petition for daily bread, suggests that we need to plead for the one as often as we ask for the other. And our Father instantly and freely forgives us according to the riches of His grace. He is only too ready to forgive. He yearns over the wayward and stubborn, who keep their faces averted from His. He sorrows for their sins; but sorrows most of all that they will not take the only position in which His tender, forgiving grace can come to them.

As the hungry sea frets down the line of cliff to find an aperture through which to pour itself, and seethes and sobs until it finds room, so does the love of God wait impatiently outside our hearts till we open to it in confession and repentance. Then God forgives, not meagrely or stintingly, but royally, gracefully, abundantly. His forgiveness is worthy of Himself, proportioned to the wealth of His glorious being, and according to the riches of His grace. He does more than forgive; He "remembers no more". He does more than forget: He sets the joybells ringing, and cries, "Let us make merry". He does more than this: He insets the scars of our sins with jewels —where sin abounded his grace abounds much more—

and all because of the Blood that has set free this wealth of mercy.

1 : 18.

God indwells us with the riches of his glory.

His inheritance in the saints is not what they have in God, but what God has in them. "The Lord is the portion of my soul" is one side of the truth; but "the Lord's portion is His people, Jacob is the lot of his inheritance" is the other, and is equally important. We settle on the nature of God as our estate, living on its abundant crop, and mining for its hidden treasures; and God comes into possession of us, as a man might of an estate which had lain for long years exhausted and barren.

Ah, what gladness rings through the deserted acres when the tidings fly from hedge to hedge, and from field to field, as though the birds carried them, that one has come into possession who is well able to pour in tons of enriching soil; and to continue doing so for long years, if need be, until corn replaces weeds, fir-trees thorns, and myrtle-trees briars. It may be that some soul, reading these lines, is sick at heart, and cries, "I am that barren thorn-cursed soil." Nevertheless, lift up thy head and rejoice! for the Lord has come in to dwell, never to depart; and He will do great things. He will create all that He commands. He will put in what He calls out. He will pour into thee wealth on wealth; as though a millionaire should put ten fortunes into an unproductive mine. He will make thee know the riches of the glory of his indwelling in the heart; and He will not forsake thee until the revenues of thy life begin to repay Him in love and adoration. But of this we shall have more to say ere this treatise has reached its close. (see Chapter 14).

17

2 : 4—8.

We are monuments of God's wealth.

That He could love us when we were dead like Lazarus, in trespasses and sins; that He has linked us in the bonds of indissoluble union with his Son; that He has made it possible for us to share His resurrection, His Triumph, and His Throne; that we, the poor children of earth and sin, should be admitted into the inner circle of Deity—*this* will be, to all eternity, the mightiest proof of the exceeding riches of his grace.

The word "exceeding" might be rendered "beyond throwing distance." Fling your thoughts forward as far as you can, and there will always be an immense *beyond*; throw them as high as you may, till they outsoar the stars, and there will always be an *above*; let them sink for ever, and there will always be a *beneath*—in the exceeding riches of God's grace.

"The heavens declare the glory of God, and the firmament showeth His handiwork"; but the glory of the position and character of the saints, contrasted with the degradation from which they were raised, will be accounted in coming ages a more extraordinary exemplification of the riches of Divine grace than the splendour of the heavens is of the wealth of his skill.

3 : 8.

God's wealth is for all.

The special note of this Epistle, and of that to the Colossians, is Paul's desire to express his conviction of the universality of God's bounty. It is not for Jews only, but for Gentiles. His commission was to preach among the *Gentiles* the unsearchable riches of Christ. The mine is inexhaustible; in it are the precious things of heaven above, and of the depth beneath, of the fruits of the sun, of the fulness of the earth, of the abundance of the seas, and of the hidden treasures of the sand: and it is all for *all* who believe.

3:16.

Our strength may be in proportion to our Father's wealth.

Who is there of us all that does not long for strength, whether to suffer or to do? The sapling says, "Let me be strong, to bear the harvest of the rich autumn fruit." The child says, "Let me be strong, that I may help mother carry her burdens, and do her work." The invalid says, "Let me be strong, that I may tread again the heather, and roam the woods, and carry light into darkened homes." "Let me be strong," the Christian cries, "that I may not faint nor be weary; that I may launch the Master's boat; or that I may gather in the golden sheaves." Who would not wish to be strong for His sake. who speaks as a Lamb from the Throne?

The strength of God awaits us, through His Spirit pouring into the inward man. Reader, I implore you, in moments of weakness and discouragement, to appropriate that strength in that measure; but remember that it is only perfected in weakness, and consummated in them that have no might.

3

"In Him"

The sponge, as it expands in its native seas, is in the clear
warm water; and the water is in it. Thus there is a
double *In-ness* between the Lord and the soul that loves
Him. He is in the believer, as the sap is in the vine, and
the spirit of energetic life in the body. But, in a very deep
and blessed sense the believer is in Christ. Of each of
these sides of this marvellous truth there are many illus-
trations in this Epistle, so specially devoted to the study
of the preposition *in*. We are dealing now with those
passages only that assure us, as believers, of being *in the
Beloved.*

1 : 3, 4, 9, 11.

(1) *We are in Christ, in the Father's Thought.*

The disclosures made to the apostle Paul of God's
hidden things—hidden from ages and generations—are
perfectly overwhelming. He tells us that our connection
with Christ, in the thought of God, is not a matter of
yesterday, nor of the day before, but of eternity.

The foundations of the earth were not laid in a day.
But, ere the aeons of creation began to revolve in their
vast cycles, before the earth or the world was formed,
God chose us in Christ. He chose Christ, and all those
who, down the far vista of time, should answer to the

attraction of his Spirit and become one with Him in a living faith.

How startling it would be if, according to a suggestion made by another, the geologist, mining deeply into the earth, should suddenly find, amid the footprints of animals long extinct, the initials of his own name cut in the primeval rock! How came those initials there? They must have been graven by the finger of the Creator! Ah, what a rush of awe would fill the breast! But a greater marvel than this awaits us here. For we learn that our names were engraven on the breastplate of the great High Priest before the amethyst or jacinth was wrought in the laboratory of Nature, among her oldest and rarest treasures.

Is there a doubt that we shall be ultimately holy and without blemish, when the stream that is to bear us thither started in eternal ages from the Father's heart? Let us at least get comfort from the thought that He who foreordained works all things after the counsel of his will.

2:10.

But the eternal purpose does not exhaust the marvels of this revelation. "We were created in Christ Jesus." It is as if the conception of the Man Christ Jesus, the Head, with the redeemed as his body, were an eternal thought in the mind of God. It is as if they were created in the thought and purpose of God, long ages ere they took shape in mortal form. It is as if the new creation were already accomplished in the intention of Him who calls things that are not as though they were. In His book all Christ's members were written when as yet there was none of them.

2:6.

We were in Christ also amid the marvels of his death.

In Him we paid the debt: in Him we lay in the grave, and broke from death, and sped on the heavenly track home to the bosom of God. In Him we sat down at the right hand of the Majesty on High, and sit there still.

3:9—11.

Time is the elaboration in actual fact of the thoughts and purposes of God. Slowly the Divine conception has taken shape in the formation and education of the Church; just as of old it took shape in the making of the world. And it is a great help to us to catch a glimpse of the direction of the Divine movement. The explorer who, from a commanding headland, is able to descry the set or lie of a country, confers a lasting benefit on all who follow him; and it is one of the inestimable benefits of revelation that it removes the obscurity which drapes our mortal lives so closely, and makes *all men see* the dispensation of the mystery.

1 : 3, 6, 7, 13.

(2) *In Christ the blessings of redemption are stored.*

All conceivable spiritual blessings needed by us for living a holy and useful life are stored in Jesus. We must therefore be in Him by a living faith to partake of them; as a child must be in the home, to participate in the provisions of the father's care. It is only they who know the meaning of the life hidden with Christ in God, and who abide in Christ, to whom God gives the key of His granary, and says, "Go in, and take what you will."

How can mortal man exhaust the wonderful gifts of our Father's grace? But they are all freely bestowed in the Beloved, in whom we also stand accepted. Who can estimate the meaning of redemption, which begins with the forgiveness of our trespasses, and ends in the rapture of the sapphire throne? But it is to be found only in Him and through His blood. What do we not owe to the sealing of the Spirit, by which our softened hearts get the impress of the Saviour's beloved face, and are kept safe until He comes to claim us? But the sealing is only possible to those who are in Him. All things are ours, but only when we are in Christ.

1:1; 3:17.

(3) *We are in Christ as the sphere of daily life and experience.*

It is the intention of God that we who believe should ever live in Christ Jesus, as the very element and atmosphere of our life; never travelling beyond the golden limits established by His Love, or Life, or Light: in Him as the root in the soil, or as the foundation in the rock. Always in His *love*, because never permitting in speech or act what is inconsistent with it. Always in His *life*, because ordering our activities by the laws of His being. Always in His *light*, because saturated by his bright purity, and illumined by His gentle wisdom. Oh to be always one of the faithful in Christ Jesus, and to be able to say with the Psalmist, "I have no good beyond Thee"! (Psa. 16:2, R.V.).

2:18; 4:21; 5:20; 6:10.

Then it would be easy at any moment to have access with boldness into the presence of God, confident that what we asked was according to his mind to give. *Then* we should sit at his feet, and be taught in Him, even as the truth is in Jesus, learning the secret of putting away the old man and putting on the new. *Then* it would not be so hard always to give thanks for all things in His name. An artesian well, fed from Heaven's deep joy, would *then* make perennial gladness in our hearts. *Then* we should never lack strength, our slender supply being fed from His Almightiness, on which we could draw perpetually. Spirit of God—Divine Anointing which we have received of Him—teach us concerning all things, and especially how to abide in Christ (1 John 2:27).

1:10.

(4) *In Christ as the centre of unity.*

It is the evident purpose of God to finish as He began. He began by choosing us in Christ. He will end by summing up all things in Him, both the things in the heavens and the things upon the earth. All the landscape focuses in the eye; all creation finds its apex in man; and all the story of the ages shall be consummated in our Lord, the Divine Man.

2:13, 15, 21; 3:6.

That unification is now in progress. The sheep are gathering up the mountainsides to stand together as one flock, beneath the care of the one Shepherd. Those who were far off are being reconciled, because the middle wall has been broken down. Those who were strangers and foreigners are recognising each other as fellow-members, fellow-partakers of the promise, and fellow-heirs. Amid the many churches, the one Church, which Jesus purchased with his blood, is being formed. From the ruins of many structures the one Temple is being built.

4

"Created In Him"

Create is one of the great words of the Bible. It is its peculiar possession. Other religious books have their cosmogonies, and attempt to explain how all things came to be. The process of production is traced as far back as possible; but they dare not speak this wonderful word. It is left to the Bible to inscribe the name of God on all things visible and invisible, and append to it the word *create*. "In the beginning God." "In the beginning God created."

2:10.

It is, however, not with the material but with the spiritual creation that we have to deal.

When we first knelt at the Cross of the Lord Jesus, we were made new creatures. "If any man is in Christ, there is a new creation; the old things are passed away, behold they are become new" (2 Cor. 5:17, R.V., *marg.*).

But there was an older creation than that. If we read aright the apostle's thought, he takes us back, beyond the limits of our mortal life, to the eternal past, and reveals to us the workings of God's thought before even the earth or the world was made. We were created in Christ Jesus, in the purpose and intention of God, before an angel sped through the newly-created ether, or a seraph raised his first sonnet of adoration. Our creation at the

27

Cross was the realization in our experience of an eternal thought of God.

Let us ponder deeply the Divine purpose in thus creating us in Christ. It was *unto good works*. The apostle was eager to put these in their legitimate and proper place. There was apparently a tendency among the converts whom he addressed to associate their salvation with their works, or, at the least, to get credit for their faith. He therefore reaffirms our entire indebtedness to grace, and says that even our faith is not of ourselves, it is the gift of God; "not of works, that no man should glory." We are not to work up to the new life, but from it. The good works we do before regeneration are not even reckoned to our account. The apostle calls them *dead* works. They are the automatic convulsive movements of a corpse. The only works that please God, and are accepted through the mediation of Christ, are those which emanate from that new life which He imparts in regeneration by the Holy Ghost. We are *created* unto good works. "He gave Himself for us, that He might redeem us from all iniquity, and purify unto Himself a people for his own possession, zealous of good works." Cain's gift of fruit may be both fair and fragrant; but it is rejected because it is an attempt to purchase God's favour, instead of being the outcome and flower of his faith.

It is very blessed to know that our good works have been prepared for us to walk in. Walking implies a *path*, whether through the cornfield, or over the stretch of moorland, or beside the sea; and we may think, therefore, of our life-course as a path which starts from the Cross, where we entered on our real life, and ends, as Christian's did, at the gate of the Golden City.

All the paths begin and end at the same points; but how different their character! and how different the character of the same path at different places! Sometimes a bit of greensward, where at every step the foot sinks deep in flowers; then a few miles of rough walking over jagged flints, which cut the feet; then a climb up the Hill Difficulty, in the face of the pitiless blast; and finally a descent into the Valley of the Shadow. Now we shiver amid the snows of the mountains; and again we are enervated by the scorching heat of the plains. At times we come into the midst of congenial companions, and enjoy their blessed fellowship in the Gospel; at other times we are carried into loneliness and isolation, and the work itself tries us to the uttermost.

But when once we have learned to believe that the pathway of our good works was before prepared for us by God; that He created for us the prepared path, endowing us with all the qualities it might demand; and that He prepared the path for us whom He created, in order to afford scope for our special powers—we come to rest in the perfect adaptation between God's creations and his preparations. Fear not: go forward! He gives what He commands, and then commands what He wills.

What relief is here!

We have no longer to choose our pathway; or cut it through the thick undergrowth of the forest; or to scheme it through the trackless waste. It is all prepared, and we have but to walk in it, with God, one step at a time. Put your hand into God's, look up into his face, saying, "Lead me, Father, in the prepared way;" "Teach me thy way;" "Make me to know the way wherein I should walk."

What confidence is here!

The only serious matter is to discover the prepared path. We may do this by abiding fellowship with the Spirit. Remember how when Paul essayed to turn aside from the prepared path of his life, and to go first to the left to Ephesus and then to the right into Bithynia, in each case the Spirit of Jesus suffered him not. For the most part the trend of daily circumstance will indicate the prepared path; but whenever we come to a standstill, puzzled to know which path to take of three or four that converge at a given point, let us stand still and consider the matter, asking God to speak to us through our judgment, and to bar every path but the right.

When once the decision is made, let us never look back. Let us never dare to suppose that God could fail them that trust Him, or permit them to make a mistake. If difficulties arise, they do not prove us to be wrong; and probably they are less by this path than they would have been by any other. Go forward!—the way has been prepared. The mountains are a way; the rivers have fords; the lions are chained; the very waves shall yield a path; the desert shall be a highway to the land which flows with milk and honey.

What scope for love is here!

Envy and jealousy need have no place. God has prepared the path for each of us, according to His infinite wisdom and love. One way is adapted for one, and another for another. Peter is girded and carried whither he would not go; whilst John tarries until the Master comes for him in the peaceful decease of old age. "What is that to thee? Follow thou Me." Each, then, can take a loving interest in the life-plan of another, sure that nothing can interfere with the evolution of his own, save his indolence or sin. Prepare us, O God, for all that Thou hast prepared for us. We will not be ambitious of great things, but to walk, day by day, humbly with Thee, and so fulfil our course. Thus shall we become thy workmanship.

2:9.

The revelation of the purpose of the Creator.

The purposes of God have been hidden deep in unfathomable mines. From the first He knew that man would fall from his high estate; but He ordained that his purpose should still be executed of making man His son, His heir, the sharer of His glorious life. Yes, and further: He resolved that his dealings with redeemed men should bring out into clearer relief his own manifold wisdom.

So he created all things through Jesus Christ. The entire fabric of creation was based upon the Person and workmanship of our blessed Lord. He was the medium and organ through whom the creative purpose moved; just as He became that through which the redemptive purpose passed into execution.

For long ages the purposes of God were obscured. Men could not tell their drift, until the Spirit of Pentecost made them understand something of the marvellous design. The mystery, which in other generations was not made known unto the sons of men, was revealed to the holy apostles and prophets in the Spirit. And now all babes who are Spirit-taught, know things which the great and good of previous ages failed to discern.

And when the completed Church stands before the assembled universe, the principalities and powers of the heavenlies will understand the manifold wisdom of God. To use the figure suggested by the Greek, then will the Church, like a prism, break into a spray of sevenfold colour, the single ray of the Divine wisdom. What a moment that will be, when God vindicates His dealings with individuals and the race!

5

"The Heavenly Places"

In his conversation with Nicodemus, while the night-breeze played over the sleeping city, coming and going as it would, our Lord spoke of Himself as being already in heaven. His bodily presence was evidently in the chamber of that house in Jerusalem, robed in the simple peasant garb which his mother had spun for Him; but in spirit, He was much more really in heaven than there. So, according to the teaching of the apostle Paul, the Church, consisting of such as believe in Christ, is really less a denizen of earth than of those heavenly places which have been entered by her Lord. They are not heaven, but heaven-like.

I : 3.

All spiritual blessings are stored there.

Human speech could never tell the infinite variety of blessings which are required for the life of the saints. Grace to endure what God sends or permits, as well as to do what He commands. So destitute are we of natural qualities and powers that we need to receive all things that pertain to life and godliness. Everything that Christ asks of us must be received from Him before it can be yielded to Him. It is therefore a source of deep heart's-ease to learn that God has stored in Jesus every spiritual blessing. As all colour lies hidden in sunlight, waiting to be drawn off by the flowers, so does help for every time of need reside in Christ.

The tense denotes a definite past act. The apostle does not say that God does or will bless; but that He *has* blessed. He carries us back into the eternal ages, in which we were created in Christ, so far as the eternal purpose is concerned, and assures us that then every conceivable blessing which we should need in our earthly pilgrimage was stored up in Christ Jesus our Lord. We have not therefore to plead for these things, as though God were unwilling to give; but humbly and reverently to lay claim to them by faith. All things are thine, O Christian soul; by which thou mayest become partaker of the Divine nature, and escape the corruption that is in the world by lust.

But since these spiritual blessings are in the heavenly places, we must live upon that plane. This is where so many mistake. They know that all the land is theirs; but they do not put their foot down upon it. We cannot inherit the treasures of the everlastir⁻ hills, whilst we are satisfied with the heavy air of the valleys. Our daily life must be spent in fellowship with the living Jesus; our thought and heart must not only ascend to Him, but continually dwell with Him; we must experimentally sit in the heavenly places ere we can claim or possess the things which God hath prepared for them that love Him.

I : 20.

Christ sits there.

It is not wonderful to find the second Person in the Holy Trinity seated far above all rule, and authority, and power, and every name that is named. But it is wonderful

34

to find him there as Man, wearing our nature, identified for ever with our race. The Mediator between God and man is Himself man (I Tim. 2:5, R.V.). The vision of Ezekiel is a literal fact—upon the likeness of the throne, which is like a sapphire stone, there is the appearance of a Man, robed in fire.

We need not, therefore, anxiously inquire what "the heavenly places" are, or where. It is enough to know that they are where Jesus is, and that they are open to us, just in proportion as we live in communion with the Lord. Abide in Him, and you are by necessity an inhabitant of these heavenly places, wherever your earthly lot may be cast. They are the hallowed meeting ground, where the saints of earth *come to* the spirits of the just made perfect. It was of them that Bunyan spake, when, describing the land of Beulah, he said, "Here they were within sight of the city they were going to; also here met them some of the inhabitants thereof, for in this land the Shining Ones commonly walked, because it was upon the borders of heaven." Only we need not locate them as always just preceding the river.

2:6.

We sit there in the purpose of God.

What Canaan was to the Jewish people, that the heavenly places are to us. When the twelve stones were taken from the bed of the Jordan and placed on the hither side, the *whole* people were deemed to have entered upon the possession of their inheritance; though as a matter of fact, two-and-a-half tribes had elected to settle on the farther side, and their wives and children would probably never cross the Jordan at all. So when Jesus passed to the throne we passed with Him.

Was He raised? So were we. Was He made to sit at the Father's right hand? *That* is our place. Was every foe made his footstool? Then not one of them can overcome us so long as we are in abiding fellowship with our risen Lord. If the "together" of the inner life is maintained, the "together" of victory is secure. Oh to tread in the power of the Holy Ghost on these high places!

3:10.

Multitudes of holy beings are there.

We know little of them. The vague term "principalities and powers in the heavenly places" veils as much as it reveals. But we shall know them one day, and be known by them. And we shall make them know the manifold wisdom and the eternal purpose of God. Here is the ministry that shall engage our redeemed energies in the land of the unsetting sun, where the flight of time is not marked, because time shall be no more. Heaven is not set out with couches and beds of ease, for our luxurious enjoyment. His servants see his face and serve. And their aim is ever to pass on to others some deeper knowledge of the being and attributes of God.

6:12.

Hosts of wicked spirits are there.

Never in this life can we escape from temptation. The holier we get, the more subtle and vehement will be the assaults of the dark legions, though they may wear white over their dusky armour. The nearer we get to our Prince in thought and fellowship, the more shall we be put to it. It is from under the opened heaven that we are driven to the wilderness to be tempted. There is no such fighting as in the heavenly places themselves. Here we wrestle not against flesh and blood, but against world-rulers of this darkness.

But the issue cannot be doubtful. In the thought of God, and in the Ascension of our blessed Lord, they are beneath our feet and conquered; and He waits to realize His purpose in the weakest of the saints. "Having done all, *stand*"; God will fight for you, and you shall hold your peace.

6

Love: On God's Side

One of the greatest words of Scripture tells us that man
was made "in the image of God." From that phrase,
throbbing with hope, we gather that our moral and
spiritual nature was planned on the same model as God's;
and that, in our original constitution, there was an
identity in quality, though not in quantity, between us
and our Creator.

This thought lies at the basis of all our reasonings
about God. If *truth*, and *holiness*, and *mercy* mean one
thing when referred to Him, and another when applied
to us, we know nothing of Him amid the blaze of
revelation and the clear teachings of our Lord. Of course,
there must always be the limitations of the finite, the
shadows of mortality falling thick and dense, the wilting
effect of sin; but nevertheless there is so great a similarity
between God and us, that we can reason from what we
know of ourselves to the nature of Him who is eternal,
immortal, and invisible.

This is specially true of *love*. We use the term of the
mysterious affinity between parent and child, friend and
friend, husband and wife. It is the strongest factor in our
nature, which bridges distance, defies time, triumphs over
impassable barriers, and irradiates with golden light prosaic
circumstances and ordinary people. We cannot explain it.
We only know that when this passion takes possession of
us, it eliminates self, and makes another's interests the

pivot of thought and effort and life. Then, turning from ourselves to God, we cry, "It is thus that God feels towards man." "God loved the world." "He loved me."

1 : 6.

God's love flows to us through the channel of the Beloved.

We must not think that the Father loves us because our Saviour interposed between His wrath and us, and made Him love us. To think this is heresy indeed. We cannot separate between the Father and the Son, for God is one. As is the Son, so is the Father. It was the one purpose of Jesus to dissipate these untrue and terrible conceptions of the Father, and to make man see that his own life and love were a true reflection of the depths of his Father's heart.

The love of God was not caused by the death of Jesus, but caused it. God did not love us because Jesus died: but Jesus died because God loved us so much as to give Him up to the death for us all. God loved us from eternity; but before His love could have its blessed way with us, it was needful for Him to satisfy the claims of a broken law, to vindicate His righteousness, to be just: and therefore He gave Himself to us in Jesus, who manifested God in the flesh, put away sin by the sacrifice of Himself, and entered into the Holiest of all to become a merciful and faithful High Priest.

Though God's love was not caused by the Beloved, it comes to us in Him. The ocean fulness pours itself through the channel of the man Christ Jesus. It has therefore all the abundance and wealth of the Divine, and all the adaptation and tenderness of the human. The

Only-begotten and Beloved Son is the reservoir in which the great love of God is stored. In proportion therefore as we abide in Him, we shall realize its blessed fulness.

2:5.

God's love was not daunted by our sin.

In the day that we were born, we were cast out in the open field, dead in trespasses and sins, and to the abhorring of our person. But He loved us even then. His great love was not diverted by the spectacle of our loathsomeness. He knew what we were, and what we should be, and how much pain and sorrow we should cost Him; but He loved us still. He foresaw our failures and backslidings, and lapses into the darkness of shadow; but none of these things availed to quench His love. So rich was He in mercy that He could afford to be prodigal of His wealth.

It is a great comfort to know that God loved us when there was nothing to attract His love; because He will not be surprised by anything He discovers in us, and He will not turn from us at those manifestations of evil which sometimes make us lose heart. He knew the worst from the first. He did not love us because we were fair, but to make us so. We cannot understand it; but since He began He will not fail nor be discouraged until He has finished his work.

3:19.

God's love in Christ passes knowledge.

We may *apprehend* it, but never *comprehend* it. We

41

may enjoy it without realizing its infinite extent; as a child may shelter in a cave from the incoming tide without being able to compute the dizzy cliffs that rise sheer above it towards heaven. A single gentian sent us by a friend gives some idea of the glory of the Alpine flowers; but how little can we imagine the effect of the myriads that make blue patches on the mountain slopes! Every time we manifest love to others we learn a little more of the love of Christ; but though we give eternity to our inquiries, His love will always pass our knowledge. The arrows will ever be beyond us. There will always be as much horizon before as behind us. And when we have been gazing on the face of Jesus for millenniums, its beauty will be as fresh and fascinating and fathomless as when we first saw it from the gate of Paradise.

Its Breadth.

It is broad as the race of man. It is like the fabled tent which, when opened in a courtyard, filled it; but when unfurled in the tented field, covered an army. It claims all souls.

Its Length.

It is timeless and changeless. It never began, it shall never stop. It cannot be tired out by our exactions or demands upon its patience.

Its Height.

Stand by the cradle, or lower yet, at the cross, and you behold it, like Jacob's ladder, reaching to the throne of God. A spiral staircase by which the guiltiest may climb from the dark dungeon into the palace.

Its Depth.

There is no sin so profound, no despondency so low,

no misery so abject, but the love of Christ is deeper. Its everlasting arms are always underneath. "If I make my bed in Hades, behold Thou art there."

As we consider these things, we can almost hear the voice of God speaking to us as to Abraham: "Lift up now thine eyes, and look from the place where thou art, northward and southward, and eastward and westward; for all the land which thou seest, to thee will I give it, and to thy seed for ever. Arise, walk through the land in the length of it, and in the breadth of it; for I will give it unto thee." When we separate ourselves from our Lots, this land is ours. It is an undiscovered continent on which we are settled; but every year we may push our fences outward to enclose more of its infinite extent.

5:2.

God's love was expressed in a supreme Sacrifice.

Wherever there is true love, there must be giving, and giving to the point of sacrifice. Love is not satisfied with giving trinkets; it must give at the cost of sacrifice: it must give blood, life, all. And it was so with the love of God. "He so loved the world, that He gave His only-begotten Son." "Christ also loved and gave Himself up. an offering and a sacrifice to God."

And this was very grateful to the Father. It was as the odour of a sweet smell, reminding us of the sweet savour offerings of the ancient Levitical code (Lev. 3:5, etc.). To us the anguish of the cross seems one awful scene of horror; but it pleased the Lord to bruise Him. In love, so measureless, so reckless of cost, for those who were naturally so unworthy of it, there was a spectacle which filled heaven with fragrance and God's heart with joy.

5:25.

God's love is as the love of the bridegroom to the bride.

In Eden man needed one to answer to him (Gen. 2:18, R.V.). There was none such among the animal creation, and his nature yearned for reciprocity of love. Then God made woman. Either sex without the other is incomplete. Together the twain are one. This is a great mystery; for our Maker is our husband, the Lord of hosts is his name. God needs us, as we need Him. The Son of God yearns for the redeemed who shall answer to Him, and give Him love for His love. Augustine said that God made us for Himself, and that we could never rest till we found rest in Him. We may reverently add that Christ Himself cannot rest satisfied until He has cleansed and sanctified the Church, and presented it to Himself in a union which eternity shall only strengthen. Ah, marvel of marvels, He wants my love! He seeks it of me, and offers His love in exchange!

6:23

God's love passes into human hearts.

"Love with faith from God the Father and the Lord Jesus Christ." The two are one. The stream issues from the common throne of God and of the Lamb; thence it flows downwards to redeemed hearts, and through them to a dying world.

Love and faith are inseparable. We trust before we love. We love, and find it easy to trust. Faith in the open channel down which God's love passes into our nature; and love in its passage hollows out the channel down which it came. Like burnished mirrors that face each other, they flash the sunbeams to and fro. And thus as we live near God we are filled with love, not ours, but His—His love reflected back on Himself—His love flung forward to men.

7

Love: On Our Side

In its deepest sense love is the perquisite of Christianity.
There is something like it, in germ, at least, outside the
school of Christ; just as wild flowers on the hedgerows
recall the rich splendour of the hothouse. But in all such
there are flaws, traces of selfishness and passion, which
prevent their realizing God's fair ideal. Love, as the Bible
uses the word, is the fruit of the Spirit. It may be grafted
on the natural stock, but it is essentially His creation.

To feel towards enemies what others feel towards
friends; to descend as rain and sunbeams on the unjust
as well as the just; to minister to those who are unpre-
possessing and repellent as others minister to the attrac-
tive and winsome; to be always the same, not subject to
moods or fancies or whims; to suffer long; to take no
account of evil; to rejoice with the truth; to bear, believe,
hope, and endure all things, never to fail—this is love,
and such love is the achievement of the Holy Spirit
alone.

1 : 4.

God's election points to his love.

Men have sometimes thought and spoken of God's
choice in such a way as to foster an exclusive and proud
conceit; as though God's election were a high wall
enclosing a favoured few, so that their flower and fruit

47

might be kept from every defiling, pilfering hand. To think this is to misconceive the entire purpose of God.

We do not deny that God has enclosed us from the great moorland waste, or that He has expended on us special pains and care; but He has not gone to this expenditure for us or for Himself so much as that the perfume of our love might be wafted afar; that we might fertilize desert places, as bees carry the pollen in their down; and that thirsty souls might be refreshed by our rare fruitage, wrought for us by the Holy Spirit. We were chosen to love—to love God above all; and to love man, made in His image.

If a man boast of his election in an arrogant and exclusive spirit, he shows that he has missed its point and aim, and is certainly outside its scope. The eternal purpose of God reveals itself, not merely in the new-found rapture, but in the new-found love. The love of God proves the election of God. If you do not love, you may prate of election as you will, but you have neither part nor lot in it. But if we are in Christ, by a living faith, we have been chosen to love, and love must be Divinely possible, nay—easy. God's choice always carries with it an equivalent of power to be and do that for which He has chosen us.

I : 15.

Love and Faith are inseparable.

When there is faith in the Lord Jesus, there will always be love toward all the saints; because faith is the faculty of taking God into the heart. Faith is God-receptiveness. Faith appropriates the nature of God; as the expanded lung does the mountain air, or as the child does the parent's gift. Faith, like a narrow channel, conveys God's ocean fullness into the lagoons of human needs. Wherever, therefore, faith links the believer to the Lord Jesus, His nature, which is love, pure as mountain dew, begins to flow *in* to the waiting, expectant heart; and then to flow *out* thence towards all the saints.

The love of God knows no favourite sect. It singles out no special school; but, as the sun and wind of nature, breathes and shines alike on all. It is cosmopolitan and universal. You cannot imprison it within the walls of any one Christian community. It laughs at your restrictions, and with equal grace raises up witnesses and standard-bearers from all parts of the Church. Thus as we become more like God, our love overleaps the barrier of our little pond and passes out to greet all saints, and to expend itself on the great world of men.

3:17.

It is only as we love that we apprehend Christ's Love.

The R.V. is very emphatic. The apostle asked that his Ephesian converts might be strengthened with power through the Spirit in the inner man; that Christ might dwell in their hearts through faith; to the end that, being rooted and grounded in love, they might be strong to apprehend, with all saints, the love of Christ. How remarkable this stress on strength! Why is it so needful in connection with love?

Is it that we should be strong to obey the least prompt-ings of the gracious Master, Christ? Is it that we need strength to suppress ourselves in favour of the new passion which has entered our hearts, until it shall have become all-powerful? Is it that the bud of Divine love in its almost perfect form can only be grafted on a strong stock? Any of these suppositions may meet the case. But we must be strengthened ere we can receive the fullness of the indwelling Lord; and one chief result of his presence within is to make us strong to apprehend his love.

Rooted in love.

The rootlets that moor a tree to the soil and gather nutriment for its growth are very slender and delicate. So the actions to which the Spirit prompts us on behalf of others may seem very trivial; but each one gives us greater constancy and strength, and makes us quicker to understand Christ's love to us.

Grounded in love.

A grounded solid foundation is all-important for the building which is to tower into the air, affording distant glimpses of the landscape; and those who desire to behold, as in a panorama, the love of God, must be content to perform many deeds of unselfish goodness in the depths of obscurity and self-forgetfulness. What we do for others for Christ's sake, and what we feel towards them, is a priceless education, preparing us to know his love. Perform loving deeds; will to do them, even if you at first shrink from them; do them from a sense of duty, if not of delight; presently you will come to delight in them, and you will say to yourself as you go to and fro, "This is something like Jesus feels towards me." Love apprehends love.

But love never lives alone. It summons *all saints* to its aid. No one saint or school of devout thinkers can compass all God's love. He who has ascended Snowdon from Llanberis must take counsel with those who left Beddgelert and Capel Curig in the early morning, that each may detail the glories he has seen; and so together they apprehend the majestic beauty of the entire mountain, as no one could of himself.

4:2, 15, 16.

Love should be the atmosphere of our church relationships.

The unity or oneness of the Spirit is a Divine reality, which we have not to make, but to keep. Try as we may, we cannot make it a whit more perfect than it is. No bases of agreement, no conferences or conventions, can do this. But we are called upon to give all diligence, that the Divine ideal may be realized, so far as possible, among the saints. There will never be uniformity; but there may be unity. The pipes in the great organ will never be all of the same length or tone; but they may be supplied by the same breath, and conspire to utter the same melody.

It must be our endeavour to guard against everything that would jar with the inner unity of the Spirit. Jealousy, bickering, harsh words, uncharitable misrepresentations— these must be under the ban of the loving soul. We must forbear one another in love.

It is often necessary to proclaim the truth, to defend it in the pulpit or the drawing-room, to enforce it to individuals to whom it may be extremely unpalatable. But love must prompt the speech and control the utterance. It is not enough to speak the truth; we must speak it in love. When a minister told the sainted McCheyne that on the previous Sunday he had preached the awful doom of the ungodly, he replied, "I hope you preached tenderly." Oh for more of the spirit of the apostle, who spoke with weeping of those that were enemies of the cross of Christ!

It is when there is perfect love between us and our

fellow-believers, that the grace of God can pass easily from one to another, through every busy point of supply, and through the working in due measure of every part. If we are out of fellowship with any, to that extent we cannot impart to them, or they to us. But when love pervades the body as the genial spring-warmth the woodlands, there is an up-building and out-flowering in love. Each gives to another, and gets as he gives.

5 : 2, 25, 28, 33.

Human love should be modelled on the Divine.

It is no ordinary love to which we are summoned. Whether in the home circle, where man and wife live in each other's presence, or in the daily walk and conversation of life, we are to imitate God, as His dear children. It is not enough to love as our fellows do. We must love as Christ did. Our one ideal must be, "as Christ loved."

To love foes, to make them friends; to love in the teeth of obloquy and shame; to love to the point of self-giving and blood; to love the foul till the pollution gives place to purity and beauty—such is the love of Christ. Let us sit at His feet and learn of Him, until we reflect Him, and are changed into the same image from glory to glory. Oh to love like Thee, blessed Master! and that we may, fill us with Thy love until our cup run over!

6 : 24.

Our love must be sincere.

There are plenty who say, "Lord, Lord," but who do not the things that He says. It is easy to be profuse in our expressions, and readily swayed by gusts of emotion, and yet to be heartless and loveless. But such do not love with sincerity. They resemble the shallow soil, where the seed soon fructifies, and as soon dies, because there is only rock beneath. For such the apostle had no words of benediction.

But wherever there is sincere love to Jesus, however weak and ignorant the disciple, there is a member of the mystical body, the Church, and one on whom our benediction may alight. You may not speak our Shibboleth or accept our creed; but if you sincerely love Jesus, we bid you welcome and wish you *grace*.

Spirit of God, baptize us in God's holy fire, that we may begin to glow with the sacred flame, and be burning ones indeed!

8

The Holy Spirit

The Holy Spirit is the special promise of the Father, made to those who are one with his Son by a living faith. "Wait," said our Lord, "for the promise of the Father, which ye heard from Me"; and immediately on His exaltation to the right hand of God He received the promise of the Holy Spirit, which He poured forth upon the suppliant Church. That promise is still open to as many as the Lord our God shall call (Acts 2:39). If, then, thou art among the called, thou mayest claim that most precious gift for thyself, and know by blessed experience "the Holy Spirit of Promise."

1:14.

He is the Seal and Earnest of our Inheritance.

Upon the yielded soul the blessed Spirit descends, bearing with Him the likeness of Jesus, which He imprints and fixes, as a stamp will leave its die upon the softened wax. Only melted gold is minted; only moistened clay is moulded; only softened wax receives the die; only broken and contrite hearts can take and keep the impress of heaven. If that is thy condition, wait beneath the pressure of the Holy Spirit; He shall leave the image of Jesus upon thee, and change thee into his likeness, from glory to glory.

This gracious operation is God's *seal* of authentication.

It is as though by an act that could not be mistaken, He said: This soul is mine—redeemed and appropriated for my own possession; and it shall be mine in the day when I make up my jewels. We place our seal on that which is unmistakably our own, and deem to be of value; so the likeness of Jesus wrought on us by the Spirit is the sign that God counts us his, and reckons us to be his peculiar treasure.

It is also the *earnest of our inheritance*. The love, and joy, and peace, which are wrought in us by the Blessed Spirit, are fragrant with the scent and beautiful with the hues of Paradise. They are the grapes of Eschol; the peaches and pomegranates of the Homeland; the first notes of angelic symphonies; the first flowers of the everlasting spring; the herald rays of a morning that shall rise to the meridian glory of a nightless day. We know that there is a land of pure delight, because we have tasted its fruits; just as Columbus knew that he was drawing near land, when the land-birds alighted on his ship, and the drift of the waves told of human habitations. Nay, more: we know, as we experience the gracious work of the Holy Spirit, the quality, though not the infinite measure, of the blessedness of heaven. The Spirit's work is not only the pledge; it is the specimen of our inheritance.

2:18.

He is the Inspirer of Prayer.

However diverse the saints are, in national birth or religious customs, they become one in the exercise of true prayer. Because as suppliants they pass into the presence of the Father through the One Mediator; and because their prayers emanate from the same Holy Paraclete.

There are two Advocates or Paracletes: one is on the throne—Jesus Christ the righteous; the second is in our hearts—the Holy Spirit (1 John 2 : 1; Rom. 8 : 26). And because He pervades all holy hearts, as the wind the variety of organ-pipes, He makes them one. Men as wide apart as Jew and Gentile have access by one Spirit unto the Father. They are therefore no more strangers, but fellows.

"If two of you agree on earth," said our Lord. The Greek word is *symphonise*. A symphony is a consonance or harmony of sounds in which there is perfect agreement. Not necessarily the same notes in different keys, but different notes in the same key. Struck by a master hand, they make delightful music. So when souls are touched by the Holy Spirit, though in many respects they differ, yet they may accord in the same prayer. Peter and Cornelius, Saul of Tarsus and Ananias, though far apart and totally diverse in temperament, respond to each other in perfect harmony. And such accord indicates the purpose of God.

2 : 21, 22.

He Indwells the Church.

Other passages clearly teach that He indwells the individual believer. He does this, that each several Christian community, fitly framed together, may grow into a holy temple in the Lord (see R.V.). The High and Holy One, who inhabits Eternity, makes His home with humble and contrite hearts. He tenants thee and me, if only we could realize it. But, in addition to this, when a company of believers is gathered in the name of Jesus, there is a habitation of God. "There am I in the midst of them."

This gives each company of disciples the mysterious power to bind and loose. Their acts receive Divine sanction, and achieve eternal results, because they are determined beneath the prompting of the Holy Spirit, and therefore in the presence of the living Saviour. The Spirit conveys the will of God to the saints, and bears back their prayers and decisions to God. Thus the Church keeps in step with Heaven, and utters, though sometimes unconsciously, the purposes of God.

3:5.

He is the Spirit of Revelation.

There are deep things of God, mysteries, hidden things, of which the apostle Paul often speaks. The eyes of the natural man cannot discern, nor his ear detect, nor his heart conceive them. Deeper than the azure depths above us, or the fathomless lakes beneath, they defy the wise and prudent of this world. But they are revealed to babes—not in the land of light and glory, but here and now, through the grace of the Holy Spirit. "God hath revealed them unto us by the Spirit."

This is what Jesus promised, that when He, the Spirit of Truth, was come, He would lead us into all the truth, and take of the things of Christ and reveal them unto us. Let us be apt pupils of so transcendent a Teacher. Be willing to do, and you shall know.

3:16.

He is the Source of Spiritual Strength.

There is no limit to the spiritual power we may receive and exercise. It is said of the Gadites that came to David, whilst he was in the hold, that the least was equal to a hundred, and the greatest to a thousand (1 Chron. 12:14). And this might be typically true of each of us. We might, like Micah, be "full of power by the Spirit of the Lord, and of judgment, and of might" (Mic. 3:8).

There is one preliminary condition, however, which we must fulfil. We must be weak enough—willing to abjure the use of those sources of success on which others boast themselves; content that the thorn in the flesh, or the test of the stream, or the wrestle at the Jabbok-ford, should reveal our utter helplessness—that the power of Christ should rest upon us. When we are weak, we shall be strong. When we are worms, God will make us new sharp threshing instruments. When we are among things that are not, God will use us to bring to nought things that are.

4:4.

He is the Secret and Source of Unity.

There is one body, the mystical body of Christ; and as the human body, in all its different organs and members, is one living unit by reason of the spirit of life that pervades it, so the Church, with its manifold diversities of organization and belief, is one, because animated by the one Holy Spirit.

Many earnest and holy men refuse outward fellowship with those who do not belong to their communion; but they are still one with them, since the Holy Spirit is in them all. And they will recognize this on the shore of Eternity.

4:30; 5:18.

We must watch carefully our own Attitude to the Holy Spirit.

He is not merely an influence; He is a person, and may easily be *grieved*. The Dove of God is very tender and gentle; and if there are thorns in the nest, He cannot remain. The things that grieve Him are instantly recognized by the holy soul by an immediate veiling of the inner light. They are enumerated here as bitterness, wrath, anger, clamour, railing, with all kinds of malice. There is no secret of the inner life more necessary than to retain the inner presence of an ungrieved Spirit.

But let us also seek to be filled by Him. We have drunk of Him, as Jesus has placed the pitcher to our lips; but we should never rest till He has become in us a spring of water, leading up to eternal life. The Holy Spirit is in every believer; but He cannot be said to fill each. There is all the difference possible between a few drops at the bottom of a bucket and a brimming well; between a few stray flowers scattered sparsely through the glade, and the myriads that make it blue with hyacinths or yellow with primroses.

To be filled with the Spirit was the blessing of Pentecost; but it awaits us all. Indeed, we are here bidden to be Spirit-filled. It is a positive command. We have no option than to obey it. Mentioned in the same paragraph with the love of husband to wife, and the obedience of child to the parent, it is as obligatory as either. Let no reader of these lines rest without seeking and receiving by faith this blessed gift, which God is able to make abound towards us. Receive it without emotion by faith: reckon it is yours: and act as if you felt it.

6:17, 18.
He is equally needful in Service and Prayer.

In conflict with Satan, whether in our own experience or in the attempt to rescue souls from his accursed thrall, there is no weapon so useful as the Spirit's sword, which is the Word of God. Our blessed Lord parried the devil's attacks by "It is written"; and we shall not improve on His method. The armour of the enemy is impenetrable to all blades save that which has been forged in the celestial fires of the Holy Spirit.

And if you would acquire the habit of intercessory and earnest prayer, so as to be able to watch thereunto, and to persevere, pouring out supplications and entreaties for all saints, you can only do so "in the Spirit." He alone can teach this holy art, or give this eager temper of soul, or perpetuate its practice. Let us earnestly seek it at His hand; for there is nothing that so refines or ennobles, purifies or strengthens the spirit, as this constant breathing in of the fulness of God.

9

"Filled"

It is said of Abraham that he died in a good old age, an old man, and *full*. It is a beautiful conception; as though all his nature had reached its complete satisfaction, and he could desire and receive nothing more. The Psalmist, too, sings of fulfilled desire; and Mary tells how God filled her hungry soul with good things. Can we speak with equal certainty of being "filled"?

I : 23.

Christ is the source of fulness to his Church and to individual souls.

We have sought to be filled with earthly goods and human love. Away upon the mountains we have essayed to hew out for ourselves cisterns, to be fed by rushing brooks and falling showers, and be always brimming; but we have been greatly disappointed. In each case a flaw or crack has made our work abortive, and we have seen the water sinking inch after inch till only drops have remained to quench the fever-flush of our souls. Not more successful have been the attempts of those who have sought rest in systems of theology, in rites and ceremonies, or in the rush of unceasing engagements. In none of these can the nature of man find its completion or fruition.

All the fulness of the Godhead dwells bodily in Him,

that of that fulness we might all receive, and grace on grace; like repeated waves that follow one another up to the furthest reaches of the tide. In Him we have been made full in the purpose and intention of God (Col. 2:9); and in Him we may be made full by the daily reception of his grace, through the operation of the Holy Spirit.

It is as if God stored the whole fulness of His nature in Jesus, that it might be readily accessible by us. The river of God, which is full of water, flows over the low threshold of His humanity, that it may be within the reach of the weakest and smallest in His kingdom. We might be afraid of the Great Spirit; but what little child, what timid woman, ever shrank from the gentle Lamb of God?

There is not one, who is in Jesus by a living faith, that may not reckon on being filled by Him. As the life-blood flows from the cistern-heart into each member and part of the body, so do the tides of life and love that emanate from the heart of Jesus pulse against the doors of all believing hearts. He fills all.

And He fills *all* in all. The heart, with its keen power of enjoyment or sorrow. The mind, with its marvellous ability of tracking the footsteps of the Creator. The sense of humour and the sense of reverence. The hours of recreation and the hours of meditation. The days of work and the days of worship. *All* in *all*.

He cannot do otherwise, without robbing or impoverishing Himself. For, as each part of the plant is needed to fill up the measure of its ideal, and as each member is required to fulfil the complete conception of a man; so each one of the members of Christ's mystical body, that Church, is essential to the manifestation of his fulness. He needs thee and me, or there will be some portion of his fulness which will never be able to manifest itself. But as sure as we present ourselves to Him, there will be an infilling of our nature with Himself, as the chill morning air, at dawn, becomes suddenly radiant with sunbeams.

3:19.

Christ's fulness is measureless.

There is no limit to the infinite nature of our Lord. The fulness of Deity is resident in Him. Only God the Father knows Him, and no other being, saint or seraph, beside. An angel with drooping wing might be imagined as reaching the furthest limit of space and be holding the last of the stars; but it is impossible to conceive of any limit whatsoever to the love, or power, or patience of Jesus. The ocean is shoreless. The height unsearchable. The depth bottomless. Such is Jesus that there is no common standard by which to compare Him with the greatest and noblest and eldest created spirit in the universe of God. You might compare such a one with the aphidæ on a leaf, for they are alike finite; but you cannot compare the finite and the infinite.

All that fulness is for us. We are settlers on the continent of Christ's infinite nature, and we are at liberty to go on putting back the walls of our enclosure, so as to take in an ever-growing share of our inheritance. But we need never fear that we shall touch its furthest limit. When we have spent a million years exploring and appropriating, we shall know as little of its real contents as the Pilgrim Fathers knew of the America which has reared itself on the foundations they laid. Though our capacities to receive out of Christ's fulness were increased a thousandfold, all their need would be as regularly and constantly met as at this present hour; because the nature of God awaits to feed them, and we may count on being filled up to the measure of the fulness of God.

That measure will always be beyond us. We may therefore rest in perfect satisfaction that we cannot exhaust it; and yet we may ever strive in our poor measure to attain more nearly towards it. The Mediterranean is ever losing volume by evaporation; and yet is always full, because it can draw by the Straits of Gibraltar on the Atlantic. And its tidelessness may well become the emblem of the peace and restfulness of that soul which has learnt the secret of taking into itself the blessedness of Jesus.

4 : 10.

This power to fill was won by Christ in his Death and Resurrection.

He did not ascend till He had first descended. Always death before resurrection; stooping before rising; the garden and the cross before the Ascension Mount.

But as surely as these come first, the others follow. He who condescended to the fashion of a man, and thence to death, even the death of the cross, must ascend by the very laws of that spiritual world which He obeyed. He could not be holden by death. "Wherefore God highly exalted Him." "Thou art worthy, for Thou wast slain."

And being by the right hand of God exalted, He received of the Father the promised plenitude of the Spirit. It had been His before, as the second Person in the Holy Trinity; but it became His now as the Representative and High Priest of His people. It was entrusted to Him as their Trustee and Surety. As we receive the fulness of forgiveness from His death, so we may receive the fulness of the Spirit from His life.

There is no soul so low in its need, but He can touch it, because He has descended into the depths of Hades; and now from the zenith throne of His ascended glory He can reach the furthest and remotest points of spiritual need: as the sun can cover a wider area when it sits regnant in the sky at noon, than when pillowing its chin upon the western wave.

4:13.

Our growth in the body is to be worthy of the head.

In a caricature you will sometimes see a large head on a very diminutive and dwarfed body; but there will be no disparity between the Head and the Body when the Divine workmanship is complete. We are diminutive and dwarfed just now; but as we abide in Him we shall grow and expand until each member of the mystical Body shall fill out to its complete proportion, and the ideal man shall stand forth before the gaze of the universe, in the measure of the stature of the fulness of Christ.

But this can only be when each joint shall supply to the whole its appropriate nutriment, and when we all give ourselves unweariedly to perfect one another in the unity of the faith, and of the knowledge of the Son of God.

5:18.

This fulness must be received.

The fulness is in Jesus, but we must *take* it. It is not enough even to pray; we must reverently and humbly *appropriate* its stores. "Give me this water," must be the

67

cry of each, "that I thirst not, neither come hither to draw."

There are three methods indicated here by which the filling process may be hastened:

1. Give yourself to holy song; if not with the lip, then in the heart, and with the music of a loving, trustful spirit, and the rhythm of a life attuned to the will of God.

2. Give thanks always for all things. Some of God's best gifts come in the roughest cases. When you see your Father's handwriting in the direction, kneel down and thank Him for the contents before you unpack them. All must be good that comes from Him.

3. Give submission and subjection to one another, except in matters that touch conscience and the demands of God.

But, above all, learn the secret of an appropriating faith, that goes to God with its need, and dips its empty pitcher down into the fulness of Jesus, and takes up at any moment of the day the supply of its thirst; not trying to feel any joy or exhilaration or emotion, but daring to believe where it cannot discern, and to act on its sure reckoning that it does receive that which it asks of God.

Too often God's ships come laden to our wharves, but we are not there to discharge them. Too often His couriers bring love letters, but we are asleep and they pass our doors. Too often His showers pass over the hills, but we do not catch their blessed fulness to fertilize and enrich our fields.

10

Power

Man longs for Power. The young man will give all he has for love; the older man counts no sacrifice too great for power. He who wields power is the idol of his fellows, even though, like the first Napoleon, he has won it at the cost of the suffering of myriads. We are not wrong in longing for spiritual power, if only we desire it for the glory of our Master and the blessing of man. It is even our duty to covet this great gift, and to take all means to procure it, that we may be strong and able to do exploits.

Let us never forget that the power of the spiritual realm is never to be had except in submission to the laws of its operation. All around us in our world-home great forces are throbbing, prepared to do our bidding, to carry our messages or draw our carriages; but we must obey them ere we can use them. Once learn the laws of their operation, and yield to them exact obedience, and there is nothing they will not do, toiling like another Hercules in notable deeds. And similarly we must learn, by prayer and watching, the laws of the operation of the power of God; that we may adapt our lives and methods to benefit by each throb and pulse of it which may be within the reach of man.

We must remember also that spiritual power is not a separate entity, which we may possess independently of the Holy Spirit. The power of the spiritual world is the indwelling and inspiration of the Holy Spirit Himself. We cannot have it apart from Him. We diminish it when He is grieved or quenched. We are most evidently the subjects and vehicles of it, when He resides in His gracious fulness in yielded and loving hearts. We covet the gift, let us then make welcome the Giver. Let us no longer speak of *it,* but of *Him.*

I : 19.

The Power of God in the Ascension Life.

We are bidden to follow our Master in his upward track, and to sit with Him, in daily happy experience, where He is already seated at the right hand of God. But this is as impossible to our unaided energy, as for the swallow to follow the majestic flight of the golden eagle, soaring sunward. So strong is the gravitation that holds us to earth, so dissipating our cares, so fickle our resolution, that nought but the Divine power and grace can lift us to the level of the Divine life.

But God waits to realize in us all that He has prepared for us; and the third item in the apostle's prayer for his converts is that they might know "the exceeding greatness of his power to us-ward who believe."

It is *power.* It is *his* power. It is *great* power: nothing less would suffice. It is *exceeding* great power, beyond the furthest cast of thought (such is the literal rendering of the word $\nu\pi\epsilon\rho\beta\alpha\lambda\lambda\omega$, employed here). It is equivalent to "the energy of the strength of His might, which He energized in Christ, when He raised Him from the dead, and seated Him at His own right hand in the heavenlies."

A marvellous lift was there! From the grave of mortality to the throne of the eternal God, who only has immortality; from the darkness of the tomb to the insufferable light; from this small world to the centre and metropolis of the universe. Open the compasses of your faith to measure this measureless abyss; and then marvel at the power which bore your Lord across it, and know that that same power is towards you, if you believe, waiting to do as much for you in your daily experience if you will but let it have its blessed way.

It is a matter of constant complaint with Christian people that they fall so far below their aspirations and hopes. They sigh at the foot of cliffs they cannot scale. The fault is with themselves. As we step into the lifts which are attached to so many factories and offices, and expect them to bear us upward, never doubting for a moment that they will do it if only we keep in the line of their ascent; so, if we would keep in abiding fellowship with the Holy Spirit—*i.e.*, if we would not wilfully step out of the range of His blessed help—we should find ourselves mounting with wings as eagles, and going from strength to strength.

3:7.

The power of God in the communication of spiritual gift.

The apostle took a very lowly view of himself. He was but a minister, a deacon, a servant; like the Master, who, when none of His disciples essayed to wash the feet of the rest, put an end to the hesitation as to who should do it, by doing it Himself. Only the greatest can stoop to these menial offices without loss of position or self-respect.

But the position that the great apostle occupied was distinctly, in his judgment, the gift of the grace of God. And he never ceased magnifying the exceeding abundance of the grace which had not only saved him, but had given him an office in the church.

The grace of God which calls us into His blessed service is connected with the energy of His power; so that whatever the work may be to which we are called, there is ever sufficient power waiting within our reach for doing it. The grace of God permits us to be His fellow-workers in the salvation of men; and the power of God moves parallel with the line of our activities, to do that which would baffle our unaided efforts. Whatever you are called to do by the grace of God, you may be enabled to do by the power of God; and you will acquire the marvellous faculty of making men see the meaning of mysteries long veiled from their view.

3 : 20.

The power of God in prayer.

In this marvellous doxology the apostle seems to have come to the limits of human speech, though not of thought or conception. Here the two seem to be on the point of parting company. The speech remains below, while the thought goes forth on its glorious way.

He had a wonderful glimpse of what God would do in answer to prayer. For notice—the power of God *without* is always commensurate with his power that works *within*. It is the same Greek word in each case. He is able to do exceedingly abundantly above our prayer or thought, according to the power that worketh in us. As I write these words, I am passing up the great Hardanger Fiord; before me rise the mighty mountains, sheer from the edge of the still green water to the snows which cool the air; the steep slopes, seamed with watercourses and covered with firs; the rock, standing forth in its naked grandeur or covered with patches of fresh green grass. But lofty and overwhelming as the mountains are, it is probable that the depth below us is equal to the height above us. So the power of God that waits to answer prayer in yonder heights, is equivalent to the power of God the Holy Ghost, who makes intercession within us with groanings that cannot be uttered.

Conceive of all that the saints have asked. Think what John Knox asked for Scotland; Luther for Germany; Brainerd and Schwartz for the heathen. Compute the agony of supplication that has been made by parents for their children; by lovers for their beloved; by patriots for their fatherland. But the God who taught them to pray was able to do exceeding abundantly above all.

Conceive of all that the saints have thought. Imagine the unspoken prayers of the saints. Things that could not be uttered because speech failed; thoughts that have flashed to and fro between the Father and his children, like love glances between those who can read each other's heart through the eyes. But God who inspired them, was able to do exceeding abundantly above all.

Above all.

He is not niggard, or scanty in his gifts, ekeing out their measure by stretching them, just coming up to the brink of our emptiness, just topping the Himalayas of our sin. Where sin abounds His grace much more abounds. He not only feeds our hunger, but gives us twelve baskets full of fragments over and above.

Abundantly above all.

We think of the profusion of spring flowers with which

He carpets the glades; of the star-dust, collected in wreaths of light on the midnight sky; of the wealth of His creative fancy in every corner of the world around us. Ah, how prolific His thought, how rich His imagination, how fertile His power! Such is our Father in nature. Think, then, O child of His, what He will not be to thee, whom He loves as He loves His Son! Ask great things of Him for His work and His world; and believe that He will far exceed thy furthest reach of desire. Thy least word will stir and bring down a blessing, mighty as an avalanche, but as soft as summer rain.

Exceeding abundantly.

We will stay here. The words cease to mean more than we have already learned. Our faculties are too immature and limited to understand their depth of meaning. Only let us yield our hearts more to the power that waits to strive and yearn within them, that the depth within may cry to the depth above.

6:10.

The Power of God equipping us for conflict.

We are seated with Christ above the power of the enemy, but we are still assailed by it in our daily experience. We wrestle not against flesh and blood, but against principalities and powers. The darkness of the world, and especially of heathen lands, is the vail beneath which malignant and mighty spirits set themselves against the Lord, and against His Christ. What are we, that we may hope to prevail, either in our own temptations, or in our efforts to dislodge them from human wills, unless we have learnt to be empowered in the Lord, and in the strength of His might?

By his own conflicts, and notably by the mighty act of His Ascension, our Lord Jesus has become, in His human and representative capacity, the storehouse of spiritual force, which has proved itself more than a match for all the power and craft of Satan. He holds in Himself a plenitude of spiritual power, which is destined finally to issue in the binding of Satan and the destruction of his realm. That power is not yet exerted to its full measure. But it is nevertheless in Him, and in Him for us. We may be strengthened with might by His Spirit in the inner man (3:16). We may become strong in the Lord, and in the power of His might; and able to do all things through Christ that strengtheneth us.

II

"The Church"

No congregation, or set of congregations, can realize the
sublime conception of the Church that rises before our
vision in Ephesians. It is as if the apostle had been able
to anticipate the glorious spectacle which John beheld in
apocalyptic vision. Though he had founded more churches
in the great cities of the Empire than any man of the
apostolic band, yet none of these alone, nor all of them
together, could realize his fair ideal of that one mystical
body, the Church, the Bride, the Lamb's wife.

This Epistle is pre-eminently the Epistle of the Church;
and the view held by men of the conception of it here
presented, will largely indicate their mental and spiritual
attitude towards their fellow Christians. There is no test
like this. We must enter into God's thought when we
speak about the Church; not as she now is, in broken
bits, like a number of squares of painted glass lying in
heaps at the foot of what is to be a window of marvellous beauty; but as she is to be when the mystery of God
is finished, and she is presented to His Son, worthy to
"answer to" Him, according to the ancient word of the
Creator, when seeking a bride for Adam (Gen. 2:18,
R.V., *marg.*).

I : 22.
The Church is a Body of which Christ is Head.

We repeat such words without emotion now; but

77

there was a time when they could not be uttered save at the cost of much that men hold dear. It is as if we were passing over a battle-field, once raked with shell and soaked with gore; or were handling a banner torn and ragged, around which the conflicting foemen fought for half a day. Let us not forget the brave hearts that were harried to death amid the heather and gorse of Scotland, rather than confess that any but Christ might assume this august title.

The Church, as a whole, must take its commands for suffering or warfare from no other lips than Christ's. Whatever course may be dictated by expediency, policy, or human leadership, she dare not move until Christ gives the signal. But if He bids her advance, protest, or suffer, she has no option but to obey. Though every voice that can reach her may be raised in expostulation and warning, she dare heed none but His.

This position of our Lord is as much for each member of the Church as for the whole Body. Because as in the natural body each several muscle, nerve, and vein, as well as the more prominent members, have direct double communication with the head, from which they derive their unity, direction, and energy; so in the spiritual Body of which Christ is head, there is not one single redeemed spirit that is not connected directly with its Lord. It would not be in the Church at all if that relationship had not first been formed. We are related to one another, only because we are related to Him. We are first members of Christ, then members of each other in Him. First Christ, then the Church.

Each member is united to the head by the *afferent* nerves that carry impressions from the surface of the body to the head; and there is nothing which happens to any one of us which is not instantly communicated to our Saviour. In all our affliction He is afflicted; He bears our griefs and carries our sorrows; He is touched with the feeling of our infirmity. The glory with which He is surrounded does not act like an insulating barrier to intercept the thrill of pain or joy that passes instantly from the weakest and meanest of His members to Himself.

Each member is united to the head by the *efferent* nerves, that carry volitions from the imperial court of the brain to the extremities of the body—withdrawing the foot from the thorn, or compelling the hand to plunge into the flame. Thus should we receive the impulses of our life from Jesus Christ; not acting on self-prompted energy, or following our own plans, thinking our own thoughts, or doing our own works, but ever subordinated to His will.

In ch. 5:23 the headship of Christ to His Church is compared to that between husband and wife; and we are reminded of one of those deep verses that reveal the unities of creation as they were present to the apostle's thought. As God is the head of Christ, the glorified Man, and as man is meant to be the head of woman, so is Christ head of each redeemed man, as an individual, and of all such together, in the Church. Thus amid the discord and anarchy of creation we are learning the Divine concords, and shall yet find harmony emanating from the Church to soothe, and still, and unify creation.

2:21.

The Church is also a Building.

Deep in the weltering floods that surged around the Cross, God laid the foundation stone which none but He could lay, which is Jesus Christ. He had laid it in purpose before He set the foundations of the hills, but He laid it then in fact. On Him souls have been built through the ages, one by one. They were lifeless indeed when they first touched Him; but coming in contact with the Living Stone, though dead they began to live, and thus the building grew.

A building is for an inmate; and the Church is for God. Without Him it has no reason to exist. The universe itself cannot contain Him; but the spiritual house whose stones are redeemed souls is His pavilion, His habitation, His home.

3 : 10.

It is through the Church that God's Wisdom is made known.

Men learn God's manifold wisdom in creation: in the limpet whose fragile shell may be pierced by a tiny insect, yet resists the blow of the mightiest wave; in the eye that is able to adjust itself immediately to the waxing or waning light; in the hand, so marvellously adapted to its myriad purposes, that the study of its manipulating dexterity has before now convinced infidelity of the being of God. But angels learn the manifold wisdom of God by studying the adaptation of His grace to the varied needs of His saints. As students discover the wonderful resources of the surgeon, who passes through the wards of the hospital adapting himself to the need of each sufferer; so do angels and the lofty spirits of heaven learn secrets they had never known, but for the infinite variety of sin and need and sorrow with which God has to deal, and which become so many prisms to break up the white ray of His character into its varied constituent hues.

The Church's end is the glory of God.

At the close of this sublime doxology, in which the burning heart of the apostle rises to an almost unparalleled ecstasy of thought and expression, he seeks for voices that shall give utterance to the glory which is the due of such a God. And, according to the Revised Version. which accurately renders the best reading of the original Greek, he finds them in the Church and in Christ Jesus. "Unto Him be glory in the Church and in Christ Jesus."

The juxtaposition of these two is very wonderful and suggestive. The thought seems to be passing from the comparison between the Church and a building or body, to trace a parallel between it and the bride, lifted by the love of the bridegroom to stand beside Him, on the same level with Himself. We know, of course, that glory must accrue to the Father, for ever and ever, from the work of the Lord Jesus. A revenue of glory will ever ascend from the cradle, the cross, the grave. The ages are to see repeated harvests accruing from the sowing of His tears and blood. But we had not realized, except for these words, that a similar wealth of glory was to accrue from the Church of the Firstborn.

Nevertheless, though our thought staggers with the conception, let us accept with reverent joy the assurance that in that great life which is opening before us, the Church of the redeemed shall stand beside Christ, and raise her voice, in unison with His, as the voice of one ascribing glory to the Father. And as the ages pass, they shall not diminish, but increase, the sweetness of her song and the volume of her voice.

4:4.

The Church is one.

A sevenfold bond of unity makes her so. One Head; one indwelling Spirit; one blessed Hope; one Lord; one Faith; one Baptism; one God and Father. She is therefore one. Her members are scattered through heaven and earth. They are to be found in many different Christian communities and sects, or belonging to none. They may ignore one another, or even refuse fellowship, because blinded to their true kindred; as two brothers may meet in a mist and not know each other. But they are one; and in the light of eternity they shall recognize the unity, for it shall be patent to all the universe of God.

5:32.

The love of Christ to his Church is inexpressible, save by the tenderest human relationship.

Here is a mystery indeed. That scene in Eden is also a parable. It was not good for Christ to be alone. He needed one to love and to give love. But there was none among unfallen angels that could answer to Him. And therefore God the Father sought a bride for his Son from among the children of men; yea, He took the Second Eve from the wounded side of the Second Man, as He lay asleep in the garden-grave.

Redeemed men compose that bride. The Saviour loves them, as a true man who for the first time loves a pure and noble woman. He does not love them because they are fair, but to make them so. He has approved His love by becoming man, and giving Himself to death. By His blood, and Word, and Spirit, He is sanctifying and purifying them for Himself. The process is long and severe; but He nourishes and cherishes them, as a man does his wounded flesh. And ere long, when the bride is complete in numbers and in beauty, the mystery that now veils her shall be flung aside, and amid the joy of creation, He will present her to Himself without spot or wrinkle or any such thing; bearing His name, sharing His rank, and position, and wealth, and power, and glory, for ever and ever.

Then the Church shall cleave to Him for ever, and He shall cleave to her. And they twain shall be one spirit. And His own prayer shall be realized, offered on the eve of His agony and passion, "The glory which Thou hast given Me, I have given unto them; that they may be one, even as We are one."

12

The Reciprocal Inheritance

Throughout the Old Testament there runs the double thought of our inheritance in God, and God's in us. And, as we shall see, this two-fold aspect of one deep conception interpenetrates the heart of the apostle's teaching in this epistle (Psa. 16:5, 6; Deut. 32:9).

1:14.

Inheritance and Inherited.

In the opening paragraph of this Epistle the apostle works up to this as his climax, that the Holy Spirit is given to us as the earnest of *our* inheritance. And, obviously, inasmuch as God is the earnest, nothing less than God can be the inheritance. In the same verse the apostle describes the saints as God's possession, which is not yet fully acquired by Him, though fully purchased; but which is awaiting its full occupation in that day of glory, when not a fragment of the purchase of Calvary shall be left in the power of the grave, but body, soul, and spirit shall be raised in the likeness of the glorified Saviour.

In the first clause of this verse. he therefore speaks of that inheritance which is ours as heirs of God, and joint-heirs with Christ. In the second, he speaks of ourselves as that inheritance upon which the Son of God so set His heart, as to be willing to obtain it by the sacrifice of the glory that He had with the Father before the worlds were made. We are therefore in turn *inheritors* and an *inheritance*.

1:14; 5:5.

The Saints' inheritance in God.

When an emigrant first received the title-deeds of the broad lands made over to him in the far West, he has no conception, as he descends the steps of the Government office and passes into the crowd, of all that has been conveyed to him in the schedule of parchment. And, though acres vast enough to make an English county are in his possession, rich and loamy soil, or stored with mines of ore, yet he is not sensibly the richer. For long days he travels towards his inheritance and presently pitches his flimsy shanty upon its borders. But even though he has reached it, several years must pass before he can understand its value, or compel it to minister, with all its products, to his need.

O child of God, thy estate has been procured at the cost of blood and tears; but thou didst not buy it! Its broad acres have been made over to thee by deed of gift. They became thine in the council chamber of eternity, when the Father gave Himself to thee in Jesus. And they became thine in fact, when thou wast born at the foot of the cross. As soon as thou didst open thine eyes to behold the crucified Lord, thou didst all unconsciously become heir to the lengths and breadths, and depths, and heights of God!

No sooner has the emigrant reached his estate, than he commences to *prospect* it. He makes a circuit of its bounds; he ascends its loftiest hills; he crosses and re-crosses it, that he may know all that has come into his

86

ownership. And this is God's message to thee, O Christian soul! Look from the place where thou art, northward, and southward, and eastward, and westward; for all this land is given to thee! Precious things of the sun and of the moon, for God is light; of the ancient mountains of His faithfulness, and the everlasting hills of His truth; of the fountains and books of His love, that gush spontaneously forth to satisfy and enrich.

But next to this, the emigrant encloses some small part of his inheritance, placing around it a tentative fence or partition; and here he begins to expend toil and skill. The giant trees are cut down; and their roots burnt out, or extracted by a team of horses. The unaccustomed soil is brought beneath the yoke of the plough. The grass-land yields pasture to the cattle; and there is not a square inch of the enclosed territory that does not minister to the needs of the new proprietor. But not content with this, in the following year he pushes his fences back further into the depth of prairie or forest, and again renews his efforts to compel the land to yield him her secret stores. Year after year the process is repeated, until, perhaps when twenty years have come and gone, the fences are needed no longer, because the extent of occupation is commensurate with the extent of the original purchase.

Let every reader mark this, that supposing two men obtained a grant of an equal number of acres, if other things were equal, their wealth would be in exact proportion to the amount of use which each had made of his special acres. If one had learnt a swifter art of appropriating the wealth that lay open to his hand, he would be actually, though perhaps not potentially, richer than his neighbour. All of which is a parable.

The difference that obtains between Christians is not one of grace, but of the use we make of grace. That there are diversities of *gift* is manifest; and there always will be a vast difference between those who have five talents and those who have two, in the amount of work done for the kingdom of God. But as far as our inheritance of God's *grace* is concerned, there are no preferences, no step-children's portions, no arbitrary distinctions. It is not as under the laws of primo-geniture, that one child takes all, while the younger children are dismissed with meagre allowances. Each soul has the whole of God. God gives Himself to each. He cannot give more; He will not give less than Himself.

If then you would know why it is that some of God's children live lives so much fuller and richer than others, you must seek it in the differences of their appropriation of God. Some have learnt the happy art of receiving and utilizing every square inch—if we may use the expression —of that knowledge of God which has been revealed to them. They have laid all God's revealed character under contribution. They have raised harvests of bread out of the Incarnation; and vintages of blood-red grape from the scenes of Gethsemane and Calvary; and pomegranates and all manner of fruit out of the mysteries of the Ascension and the gift of the Holy Ghost. In hours of weakness they drew on God's power; in those of suffering, on his patience; in those of misunderstanding and hatred, on his vindication; in those of apparent defeat and despair, on the promises that gleam over the smoke of the battle, as the Cross before the gaze of Constantine; in death itself, on the life and immortality which find their home in the being of Jehovah.

The analogy that we have quoted, however, fails us utterly in its final working out. The emigrant at last covers his estate, its mines become exhausted, its forests levelled, its soil impoverished; but when a million years have passed, the nature of God will lie before us as utterly unexplored and unexhausted, as when the first-born son of light commenced like a Columbus in the spiritual realm to explore the contents of the illimitable continent—God.

When we were children, the map of Africa gave us a few scattered names around the coast line; but the great interior was blank. Modern maps containing the results of the explorations of Livingstone, Stanley, Burton, tell another story of river, savannah, tableland, and of myriads of inhabitants. Probably, ere long the whole will have been opened up to European civilization and commerce. But with God this shall never be. We shall never know the far-away springs of the Niles and Congos of His nature; we shall never unravel the innermost secret of his being.

1 : 18.

God's Inheritance in the saints.

What an extraordinary combination! It is a mystery that God should find His inheritance and portion in the love of men and women like ourselves. But that He should find the riches of glory in them!—this passes thought. It may, however, be explained by a piece of farming that I learnt recently. The other day, when travelling in Scotland, I was introduced to some farmers whose soil was naturally of the poorest description; and yet, in answer to my inquiries, I found that they were able to raise crops of considerable weight and value. This seemed to me very extraordinary. Out of nothing, nothing comes, is the usual rule. But they unravelled the mystery by telling me that they put in, in enriching manure, all that they took out in the days of golden harvest.

Is not this the secret of any grace or wealth there is in Christian lives? Not unto us, not unto us, but unto Thee, O Christ of God, be the glory! Whatever Thou dost get out of us, Thou must first put in. And all the crops of golden grain, all the fruits of Christian grace, are Thine from us, because Thou hast by thy blood and tears, by the sunshine of Thy love, and the rain of Thy grace, enriched natures which in themselves were arid as the desert and barren as the sand. Augustine therefore said truly, "Give what Thou commandest, and then command what Thou wilt."

But we must see to it that we keep nothing back. There must be no reserve put on any part of our being. Spirit, soul, and body must be freely yielded to the great Husbandman. We, who are God's tillage, must make no bargain with His ploughshare, and withhold no acre from the operations of His Spirit.

This is the curse of Christian living. Here is the reason why God is so little to us. We are mean enough to wish to make all we can of God, and to give Him as little as possible of ourselves. We fence off a part of ourselves for God, excluding Him from all the rest. But it is a compact that will not hold. Love will only give itself to love. The shadows of secrecy or reserve on either side will blight a friendship in which all the conditions seem perfectly adjusted. And many a life that might grow rich in its heritage of God is dwindled and marred, because it sets a limitation on God's heritage of itself.

Give all thou hast to God. As He bought, so let Him possess, everything. He will occupy and keep thee. He will bring fruit out of thy rockiest nature, as the Norwegians raise crops on every scrap of soil on their mountain slopes. He will put into thee the grace that thou shalt give back to Him in fruit. He will win for Himself a great name, as He turns thy desert places into gardens, and makes thy wildernesses blossom as the rose.

13

Man in Christ

Christ is the ideal man. Once, in the course of the ages, the plant of human nature seemed to bear a perfect flower of stainless purity and ineffable loveliness. The black touch of the world's sin could not befoul it. The storms that swept over it might strike it for a moment down to the black soil out of which it sprang, but could not bemire it. It reared itself in peerless beauty, and grows to-day fair and strong in the universe of God.

The man Christ Jesus was before the first man Adam, so far as the thought and purpose of God are concerned. When the great Potter took in hand the red clay to make a man, He made it in His own image, and after His likeness. And what could these be but the nature and lineaments of that blessed Son of His love who was His fellow—Himself? The Incarnation and Ascension were only possible on these conditions. How could the Son of God have become incarnate unless the nature He was to assume had already been made after the model of Himself? And how could our human nature be taken into the ineffable glory of the Throne, unless, in a sense, it had belonged there before the worlds were made?

But Adam fell from his original type. He shared morally in that aptness to deteriorate which runs through nature. And in his fall we all fell. All who are one with him by the bonds of natural relationship shared in that sad act of disobedience and its results. How great that fall was may be judged when we consider the wizened babes, the wretched women, the blear-eyed, soddened victims of drink and sin which abound amid the most civilized and refined cities of the world, and compare them with the Man of Nazareth, that holy thing which was born of the virgin-mother.

But Jesus is more than type. He is the second Man, the life-giving spirit; and therefore capable of repeating Himself in myriads of souls—not in His Divine essence, but in His human beauty. This is the singular power of life, possessed in common by plant and animal—the marvellous gift of reproduction. Adam begat a son in his own likeness, after his image. And the second Man possesses the same glorious power, by which He is able to fashion anew the body of our humiliation, that it may be conformed to the body of His glory, according to the working whereby He is able even to subject all things unto Himself.

2 : 15.

'*One new man.*"

When this Epistle was written, the hatred of centuries had reached its climax. The Jew, able to trace his unbroken line of descent from Abraham, proud of the religious prerogatives of his race, magnifying his unique relationship to Jehovah, looked with scorn on the uncircumcised Gentiles around. They were Gentile dogs. He spat on the ground if they crossed his path.

As long as the Mosaic ritual was the prescribed method of approaching Jehovah, there was no way of removing this hostility. The Jew entrenched himself within its barriers, justifying his hatred by religious sanctions. The Gentile chafed and rebelled against its exactions. But our Saviour, in His flesh, and by His cross, broke down the middle wall of partition, and abolished the enmity even the law of commandments contained in ordinances. He fulfilled the law so perfectly—not for Himself, but for all—that it had no more to ask. Its claims were met and satisfied; and therefore the Jews could not insist on them, on the one hand, nor the Gentiles chafe beneath them on the other.

Moreover, by His death the Saviour has made an atonement and propitiation for men as men. Not for the Jew in one way, or the Gentile in another; but for all on the same terms. By one death, in one body on the cross, which is common to the whole world of men, and by His intercession, through which both have access to the one Father, He has brought to an end the divisions of ages.

But He has done more. In His resurrection, He is constituted the origin and head of a new race. The race of regenerate men! The race of His resurrection-life and power! The race of the new heavens and the new earth. All who believe in Him are born into that new humanity. It is the one new man, which is composed of all nations, and kindreds, and peoples, and tongues.

3 : 16.

The inner man.

Beneath the play of our outward life, and beneath the workings of our busy brains, there lies a deeper self, which the apostle calls "the inner man." There is an objective and there is a subjective self. The former occupies itself with collecting impressions and thoughts from the world around, and in action or speech; but the latter, veiled from observation, muses, arranges its stores, carries on long trains of thought, holds fellowship with itself, and God, and the unseen. It is this part of our nature which perceives truth—not by trains of argument, but by the flash of intuitive perception—and which receives those throbbing pulsations of Divine power that wait around us seeking for admission.

This inner man is in us all; but many of us live in the outer courts of our nature, occupied with the mere externals of our life and the world. We give these inner chambers over to neglect and dust; seldom entering them, and hardly cognizant of their existence, save when in hours of unusual solemnity they assert themselves and compel attention.

It is in this inner man that the Spirit finds his home and seat. This is the Holy See. Here He elaborates His purposes, formulates and issues His decrees, and stirs to heroic action. And when all its avenues are open to Him, He so infills with His power, and indwells with Divine energy, that the inner man is strengthened with might, according to the riches of His glory.

4:13.

The full-grown man.

From the hands of the Ascended Saviour, gifts are distributed to His Church. He gave some, apostles; and some, prophets; and some, evangelists; and some, pastors and teachers. But to every member of the Church, the weakest and obscurest, some special grace was given, according to the measure of the gift of Christ. Every joint in the body has some function to perform to all the rest, and to the growth and perfectness of the whole.

But alas! too many of the saints are unaware of the possession of gift or gifts, or they leave them buried in a napkin in the earth, or they are out of joint, and so unable to do their specific work. The special function of the officers of the Church—the apostles, the prophets, the pastors—is to stir the saints to discover their gifts; and, if needs be, to put them into articulated union with the Lord, so that they may take up the work of ministering to the rest of the body.

This thought, which is somewhat obscured in the older version, is made abundantly clear in the Revised. "For the perfecting (the setting in joint) of the saints, unto the work of ministering, unto the building up of the body of Christ" (12).

As the piccolo may be missed out of a great orchestra; as each single joint is indispensable to the body's health and vigour; so each believer has a part to do, by thought or speech, by suffering or action, in building up the great mystical body of the Lord. Some vision of his beauty received and passed on—some deep sweet word, some trait caught from fellowship with Him and reflected from the pallid brow of sickness, some unselfish act of which the world knows nothing—such are the contributions that we make to the upbuilding of the body. We may seem to do nothing else than minister to the particles just against us, but this re-acts on the whole.

And presently—it may be nearer than we suppose— the body will have reached its full growth, will have attained to the measure of the stature of the fullness of Christ, and will be worthy of its Head. All the saints with Jesus shall make together a full-grown perfect man, which shall realize in completeness the Divine ideal.

The old man.

The old man is the aggregate of habits and methods of life, which marked us before conversion. The phrase describes the impression which we produced as men and women upon our fellows. What we were wont to be, and say, and do. That form of character and life which was ours before the great change operated through faith in Jesus.

It is called *the old man,* as if there were but one, because the habits and tastes, the thoughts and acts of men, before conversion, have much in common. There is not much to choose between them. It is one evil nature: one likeness to fallen Adam; one type of evil, though its forms are slightly modified in different temperaments and by special circumstances.

It is under the control of deceitful lusts. In other words, it is shaped by the passionate desires which have their origin in the strong natural tendencies of our being. These were given us by God to be the motive-forces of our nature, but not to rule. For when once they are permitted to usurp this position, corruption ensues, and the nature rots piecemeal before their insidious action— as the body of the leper beneath the living death that eats away his flesh. Ah, deceitful lusts! promising liberty, and happiness, and joy, but resembling the Syren sisters, whose upper form was fair, but whose lower extremities were foul; whilst whose sweet songs allured the unwary mariner only to ruin.

We must not defer this "putting off." The tense indicates the sudden resolve of the will, inspired and empowered by the Holy Spirit to be no longer under the dominion of these terrible passions. Once and for ever let us divest ourselves of them; as the beggar his rags, or as Lazarus the cerements of death.

4:24.

The new man.

This is the aggregate of blessed habits that mark the life of the converted—the white robe of purity, the girdle of self-restraint, the silver of humility, the jewels of holy character. All through the Epistles we are bidden to don it. "Put on the armour of light." "Put on, as God's elect, a heart of compassion." "Put on the Lord Jesus Christ."

It is *the* new man, because the habits and character of the children of God are very similar. There is a family likeness common to all. It is *after* God, because it is created in His likeness. It is the fashion of God in human nature, perfectly exemplified once in Jesus Christ, and now waiting to be imparted by the Holy Ghost. It is *righteous* toward man. It is *holy* toward God. It is *true,* perfectly transparent and sincere. Put on this holy thing! Created in Jesus, and therefore not to be woven by human effort or spun by outward obedience to rites, but to be simply assumed.

Put it on by faith. Do not try to build up Christlikeness by your repeated endeavours. Just assume it by faith. Believe it is yours. Reckon that it is so. Go out believing that Christ's likeness is on you, and His beauty clothing you as a beautiful robe; and men shall increasingly realize that it is not you but Christ. The beauty of the Lord will be upon you; and the life of Jesus will be manifest in your mortal body, both in life and death.

14

Our Walk

Our walk is a synonym for our life. Life is a walk from the cradle to the grave. Our steps emerge from the jewelled gates of birth, traverse rock and sand, enamelled meadow and difficult mountain steeps, and ultimately pass within the portal of death, which, though sombre enough when seen from afar, is often found to be irradiate with light from the world beyond.

In this sense the word occurs in all parts of Scripture. In the opening chapters of Genesis it is said of Enoch that he *walked* with God. And in one of the last Epistles, we are bidden to *walk* even as Jesus *walked*. And between these extreme points, the pages of Holy Writ are strewn with similar references. Indeed, the comparison of life to a pilgrimage is based on the same conception. The race of man goes afoot, as a vast host.

A walk is made up of steps. Though a man circle the globe, yet he must do it by one step at a time; and the character of the steps will determine the character of the walk. So life is made up, for the most part, of trifles, of commonplaces, of the reiteration of familiar and simple acts. And what we are in these, that will be the colour and value of our lives in the verdict of eternity. Life is not made by the rapturous but brief moments which we spend on the transfiguration mount; but by the steps we take to and fro along the pathway of daily duty, and of sometimes monotonous routine.

2:2.

The walk of the old life.

The apostle does not scruple to unveil the past of those whom he addressed. "Look," he cries, "to the rock whence ye were hewn, and to the hole of the pit whence ye were digged. Ye were once dead in trespasses and sins." But though in our unconverted state we were utterly dead to the claims of God and the life of the spiritual world, yet we were very much alive to the promptings of that malign trinity of evil, which is ever set upon the ruin of the souls of men. "Ye were dead ... ye walked."

As the doctrine of the Divine Trinity is never expressly formulated in Scripture; though it may be derived from many an obvious inference, so there is no difficulty in showing that the world, the flesh, and the devil, are in essence one in their endeavour against the soul. Here, for instance, in successive sentences, the apostle speaks of "the course of this world"; of "the prince of the power of the air, the spirit that works in the sons of disobedience"; and of "the lusts of the flesh and of the mind."

Here are several points that deserve our earnest thought.

(1) Those who live a worldly life are as much under the influence of the devil, and as much children of wrath, as those who give way to the lusts of the flesh. This is a very solemn thought. We make distinctions which are not recognized by God. We classify sinners after a fashion which will not stand the test of eternity. We pity the child of fashion, whose one thought is dress, rank, and amusement; flitting like a butterfly from flower to flower, and squandering the priceless hours in vanity and gaiety. But in the sight of God, such a one stands in the same category, is the prey of the same evil

spirit, and is menaced by the same doom as the libertine or the sot. It may even be that a frivolous worldly life is more offensive to God than that which is swept by violent storms of passion.

(2) Beneath the shows of this world—its pageantry and pomp, its fascinations and ambitions, its round of amusement and engagement—there lurks the disobedient spirit, who is set upon inducing disobedience to God, and whose seat is in the air.

It is difficult to understand precisely the meaning of these words. Is "the air" a different locality to the "heavenly places"? Has the seat of the devil's kingdom been shifted from the earth or the heavenlies to the air? Is the very atmosphere laden with the invisible microbes of Satanic influence? We cannot tell. But it is enough for us to know that, while Satan tempts some through their passions, he tempts others through the riches and baubles, the shows and lures, the cares and anxieties of worldliness, which is Godlessness. This explains why the apostle John said that the love of God was not compatible with that of the world.

(3) As the Spirit of God works in those who fear to grieve Him, so the spirit of the prince of the power of the air works in the unregenerate and unbelieving. There are secret passages to our souls by which influences, whether from heaven or from hell, may enter our most secret thoughts. By the one we are prompted to crucify the flesh with its affections and lusts, that we may live unto God; by the other to indulge the desires of the flesh, and of the mind, and so to remain dead unto God, dead in trespasses and sins.

(4) It is as ruinous to the inner life to indulge the desires of the *mind* as those of the *flesh*. By the marvellous gift of imagination we may indulge unholy fancies, and throw the reins on the neck of the steeds of passion

—always stopping short of the act. No human eye follows the soul when it goes forth to dance with satyrs or to thread the labyrinthine maze of the islands of desire. It goes and returns unsuspected by the nearest. Its credit for snow-white purity is not forfeited. It is still permitted to watch among the virgins for the Bridegroom's advent. But if this practice is unjudged and unconfessed, it marks the offender a son of disobedience and a child of wrath.

It is thus that we walked once. But God loved us, and lifted us out of these dark and dangerous paths, putting us on the Ascension track; may He keep us from choosing or treading them again. Hedge up those ways with thorns, dear Lord, and make fences against us, that we may not find them.

2 : 10.

The walk of good works.

Before the vision of the evangelic prophet arose the conception of a highway that should intersect the desert. It was the way of holiness; the unclean should not pass over it. No lion or beast of prey would haunt it; none but the redeemed would tread it. As soon as they should touch it, gladness and joy would greet them like twin radiant angels; whilst sorrow and sighing, that had pursued them hitherto, would drop away disappointed, like dark angels of the pit.

That causeway was prepared for the ransomed before the foundation of the world; but it was fully opened and revealed by the work of Christ and the grace of the Holy Spirit. Directly we yield ourselves to these blessed influences, we begin to tread it. We find that each step has been prepared for us, so that we have but to put down our feet. As long as we keep it we are safe from alarm and molestation. Our hearts beat out the glad marching music to which our feet answer blithely. And sorrow and sighing flee away.

4:1.

Walk worthily of your calling.

The simplest words are the deepest. Take, for example, the word *call*. It is constantly on our lips. The shepherd's call to his sheep, the herdsman's on the hills, the mother's to her child. And God appropriates it in his dealings with men. He *calls* them. From the throne of His glory He speaks to every soul of man, once, twice, many times; as when He said "Samuel, Samuel," or "Saul, Saul." In some solemn hour of decision, in a moment of awful crisis, by human voice or written word, or by the pleading and remonstrance of conscience, God's voice may be heard calling men to Himself, to Heaven, and to a saintly life. On that call the apostle bases his argument for holiness. Act worthily of the love which summoned you, and of the goal to which you have been called. Stand still and ask yourself before you speak, or act, or decide —Is this worthy of that great ideal which God has conceived for me, when He called me from the rest of men to be his priest, his saint, his son? If not, eschew it!

4:17; 5:8.

Walk in the light.

God is light; and when we live in daily, hourly communion with Him, in such a frame of mind as that His name is frequently in our hearts, or murmured softly by our lips, or spoken as a talisman when temptation is near, we may be said to be walking in the light. And it is just in proportion as our steps tread the crystal pathway of light, that our understanding becomes enlightened. In God's light we see light. When the heart is pure, the eye is single.

The contrary to this is also true. When we are alienated from the life of God, our understanding is darkened to the truth of God. The seat of infidelity is in the heart. Once let a soul become shut out from the life of God through the hardening of the heart; once let it give itself up to lasciviousness, and to make a trade of uncleanness with greediness: then the light of the knowledge of the glory of God beats against a shuttered window, asking for admittance in vain.

If you would know God; you must resemble God. If you would learn God's secrets, you must walk with God. If you would know the doctrine, you must be willing to do his will.

But there is something even better than walking in the light; it is to become children of the light. What an exquisite conception! Dewdrops sparkling in the light of dawn; star-dust glittering on the vault of night; humming-birds flashing in the tropic sun; children dancing in light-hearted glee—none of these are so truly sons of light as they who have been begotten by the Father of Lights; who carry within them the Light that lights up hearts, and who, in goodness, righteousness, and truth, prove what is well-pleasing unto the Lord. Let us live as such.

5:2.

Walk in love.

We are to imitate God's love in Christ. The love that

gives, that counts no cost too great, and, in sacrificing itself for others, offers all to God, and does all for His sake. Such was the love of Jesus—sweet to God, as the scent of fields of new-mown grass in June; and this must be our model.

Not to those who love us, but who hate; not to those who are pleasant and agreeable, but who repel; not because our natural feelings are excited, but because we will to minister, even to the point of the cross, must our love go out. And every time we thus sacrifice ourselves to another for the sake of the love of God, we enter into some of the meaning of the sacrifice of Calvary, and there is wafted up to God the odour of a sweet smell.

5:15.

Walk carefully.

Pick your way amid the pitfalls of the world. Gird up your flowing robes with dainty care, lest they be soiled by the filth of the street. Beware of any side paths that would lead your steps away from the narrow track. Watch and pray. Especially be careful to turn every moment of time into an opportunity of making progress in the Divine life. Take heed to the moments, and the hours will take heed to themselves.

All these injunctions, however, will baffle us, and leave us stranded on the shore, when the impulse of their stimulus ebbs, unless we blend with them the thought that God is willing to walk with us—nay, *in* us; for He saith, "I will dwell in them, and walk in them." Abide in God, and God will abide in you, and walk in you, till you walk with Him in white, being found worthy.

15

The Christian Armed

Each Christian has to meet with the powers of hell, in his own life, and in his capacity as a soldier of the Gospel of Christ. It is with the latter aspect of the conflict that the apostle is specially concerned, in the last chapter of the Epistle we have been studying. We do not question that there is a reference to the personal conflict which each believer has to maintain with the principalities and powers of evil. But the stress laid on the fact that they are the world-rulers, or the rulers of the darkness of this world, is significant of that wider conflict which the Church, and each member of it, is called upon to maintain with the grim hosts of evil that lie unseen behind those systems of superstition, cruelty, and pride, which oppose the Gospel of Jesus Christ.

It is well for us to recognise this supernatural element in the evil by which our work for God is confronted, and often sorely pressed. We have to wrestle, not simply with the stupidity, barbarism, or intellectual acumen of flesh and blood, but with the spiritual hosts of wickedness which are in the heavenly places. (See Dan. 10.)

There is no need, however, for us to abate one jot of courage, for in His Ascension all these principalities and powers were put under the feet of our Redeemer; and as we abide in Him, we share His conquest; we are more than a match for the mightiest forces of hell; we walk upon our high places.

But the apostle makes it clear that we must possess certain personal qualities before we can avail ourselves of the victory or power of the Captain of our Salvation. This is what he means by urging us to put on the whole armour of God, that we may be able to withstand in the evil day, and having done all to stand. Let us ponder this; for to neglect it is the cause of much of the failure of Christian workers. They are not careful enough as to their personal character, and so the devil laughs them to scorn; for by their inconsistencies they cut the sinews of their faith and dissociate themselves from the only source of victory that he dreads. (Compare 2 Peter 1 : 5—11.)

6 : 14.

The Christian warrior must be true.

The loins are significant of strength; and girded loins represent the opposite of self-indulgence, slothful ease, or carelessness. Hence the need for the girded loin; and our Lord solemnly insists on it as a prime necessity for His servants. "Let your loins be girded about, and your lamps burning."

We must gird ourselves with truth. We must be true to the laws of our nature, never overstepping the limits of moderation, never using for self-indulgence the powers which were intended only for the maintenance of the fires of life; never yielding to that worse self which lurks in us all, as the miasma in the fairest landscapes of southern climes. We must be true to God who made and redeemed us; true to our best selves, our noblest ideals; true to those with whom we live, and who are certainly affected for good or evil by our self-restraint or the reverse.

There is the strongest obligation that we should often stand foursquare before the mirror of truth; which is Christ—Christ the Light that lighteth every man—Christ in conscience—Christ in the Word. There is no severer or straighter test than this. With unfailing accuracy we shall discover our true selves, as we come face to face with Him, who is girt with righteousness as the girdle of His reins, and faithfulness as the girdle of His loins. Let there be any obliqueness, or irregularity, or inconsistency, it will be at once and unerringly revealed. No distortion of the inner life can escape detection or condemnation before the judgment-seat, whose decisions are ratified by each soul's secret convictions of justice. Would that we were all in the habit of submitting to that faithful scrutiny—not the greater matters only. but all the smallest details of our lives!

Then let us, in the name and by the power of Jesus, put away all that has been shown to be inconsistent with His character and claims, and let us submit in everything to His control. It will cost us something. We may have difficulty with our judgment, warped and injured by self preference. We may have to contend with our will, reluctant to sign the death-warrant of some favourite habit. We may feel singularly powerless to carry into effect what we know, in our loftiest moments, to be our only safe and blessed policy. But happy are we, if we dare to catch up the trailing robes of self-indulgence, and restrain them under the cincture of inexorable truth and purity.

6:14.

The Christian warrior must be righteous.

"Put on the breastplate of righteousness." This

righteousness is not primarily that which is reckoned to us, so soon as we believe in Jesus, but rather that personal righteousness which is wrought in us by the Holy Spirit, and in virtue of which our characters are conformed to that of Jesus Christ the Righteous. The apostle refers to it when he reminds Titus that the grace of God instructs us to deny ungodliness and worldly lusts, and to live soberly, *righteously*, and Godly, in this present world. It is the temper we should cultivate and manifest in all our dealings with men. The breastplate is worn upon the heart, the seat of our affections and emotions. In these especially we must be right.

It is very necessary to remember this. Of what use is it to speak of Jesus to those who are rankling under a sense of our injustice, or are sensible of some glaring inconsistency in our character? The effect of our most eloquent entreaties is neutralized by our deeds, which speak even louder.

What a beautiful contrast there is between the laxity of too many of us and the scrupulous care of the apostle Paul! How watchfully he exercised himself to have a conscience void of offence toward man as well as God! How sensitive to the least appearance of self-seeking, that he might cut off occasion from them which desired an occasion! How gladly he went without what was in itself lawful, lest his ministry should be blamed!

It becomes the Christian to put it beyond the power of man or devil to point some inaccuracy in life or conversation, and to say, "This man belies his profession, and contradicts his own teaching." Rather let us suffer wrong, and submit to overcharge, and give men even more than they can justly claim. Anything of loss or suffering may be cheerfully met, in order that night after night we may wash our hands in innocency, and feel that we have not put a stumbling-block in the path of any man.

This is only possible as we abide by faith in Christ our righteousness. And when we have done our best, we shall have nothing to boast of. We are always unprofitable servants, who have only done what they ought.

6:15.

The Christian warrior must follow after peace.

"Your feet shod with the preparedness of the Gospel of Peace." There is undoubtedly a reference in these words to Isaiah's vision of the messengers, who, with beautiful feet, speed across the mountains to proclaim the good tidings of the Gospel. But there is the further thought, that those who carry the Gospel of Peace must tread gently and softly.

If the Gospel of Peace is our message, the peace of God should mantle our face with a holy calm; breathe through our lips like a benediction; and diffuse itself like the dew of the Lord over the places of human rivalry and hatred. Ours should be the blessedness of the peacemakers. Our tread should be only in the paths of peace, except when the trumpet of God clearly calls us to war against the sins and wrongs around. "If it be possible, as much as in *you* lieth, be at peace with all men. So then, let us follow after things which make for peace, and things whereby we may edify one another. The Lord's servant must not strive; but be gentle towards all, apt to teach, forbearing, in meekness correcting them that oppose themselves." Be it ours, then, always to be on the alert to promote peace and love amongst men; not incensed or irritated by their rancorous dealings with ourselves; not catching fire at the flame of their wrath and indignation.

6:16.

The Christian warrior must be vigorous in faith.

As each fiery dart, tipped with the flames of hellish hate, comes speeding to the soldier of the cross, deafened by the din and blinded by the smoke of battle, he must catch and quench it on the golden shield of faith, that it reach not his head or heart.

Sometimes a slander will be circulated, for which you have given no occasion; or a venomous speech or article will be hurled at you; or some horrible suggestion will be thrust between the joints of the armour; or some deadly reminder of the sins of the past, which you can never recall without burning remorse. At such times we are tempted to give back, to renounce our work, to withdraw from the battle. And those will certainly yield to the temptation, who are not inspired by the faith that can hand these things over to the compassionate and mighty Saviour, who knows all, but loves better than He knows, and who interposes to cover our heads in the day of battle.

But faith like this is only possible to him whose hands are clean, and his heart pure; who is living in daily fellowship with Jesus, and whose soul is nurtured by daily feeding on the Word of God.

6:17.

The Christian warrior must know God's salvation in his own experience.

He must be saved from the guilt and penalty of sin before he can proclaim the plenitude of God's forgiveness to the chief of sinners. He must know the Gospel as the power of God unto salvation from the dominion of sin in his own heart. He must be anticipating the consummation of God's purpose in the redemption of the body. As the helmet glistens in the sunshine, so must the crown of the Christian's experience point upward to heaven and onward to the glory yet to be revealed. He must speak that which he knows, and declare what he has seen and heard. It is when we are experiencing the power of God's salvation that we can declare it to others, with a freedom and a power that needs no further corroboration. And it is when men see the salvation of God exemplified in our own life and character, that they will be prepared to accept it as indeed the Word of God.

6:18.

The Christian warrior must use the two essential means of grace—the Word of God, and Prayer.

Add to all the above the diligent use of the Word of God in the culture of our souls, in the preparation of our messages, and in dealing with the conscience of our hearers; and let there be besides the perpetual use of the weapon of All-prayer, and there is no enemy born of hell that shall be able to withstand us, who, in the feebleness of human weakness, are strong in the Lord, and in the power of his might.

Daily meditate on your union with the ascended Lord: reckon that in Him you have died to sin: and present your tempted members as instruments of righteousness unto Christ—and yours will be a course of unbroken victory.